CROSS-STICKING STUDIES

BY RON SPAGNARDI

EXERCISES FOR MOVING AROUND THE DRUMSET

Design and layout by Scott Bienstock

Cover illustration by Joe Weissenburger

CD produced by Michael Dawson

Published By:
Modern Drummer Publications, Inc.
12 Old Bridge Road
Cedar Grove, NJ 07009 USA

All CD tracks created in Ableton Live using FXpansion BFD2 drum software
and Modern Drummer's Snare Drum Selects, Volume 1 sample library.

Contents

	CD Track #

Introduction

Cross-sticking is the term used for moving from one drum to another with one hand *crossing over* the other, as opposed to moving from drum to drum in the conventional manner. This technique has been used by many great players over the years, such as Buddy Rich, Joe Morello, and Louie Bellson, who dazzled audiences with exciting criss-crossing motions around the kit. In fact, drummers like these performed cross-sticking maneuvers with such speed and fluency, many drum students were left baffled by what was actually being played.

Cross-Sticking Studies was designed to take the mystery out of the concept. By following the series of progressive exercises laid out here, drummers who already possess a substantial level of solo skills—but who want to add a greater degree of rhythmic and visual interest to their solo work—will better understand the technique, and develop a good measure of facility on their own.

Cross-Sticking Studies is based on four cross-sticking maneuvers that are used consistently throughout this book:

1) SNARE DRUM TO FLOOR TOM with the left hand crossing over the right.
2) FLOOR TOM TO SNARE DRUM with the right hand crossing over the left.
3) SMALL TOM TO FLOOR TOM with the left hand crossing over the right.
4) FLOOR TOM TO SMALL TOM with the right hand crossing over the left.

**All notes requiring a cross-sticking move
(right over left, or left over right) are notated with a circled X:** ⊗

Section 1 of this book presents exercises that incorporate all four cross-sticking maneuvers with 8th notes and 16th notes. Three different sticking patterns are used: Alternate Sticking, Double Sticking, and Single Paradiddles. Each part concludes with a series of two-bar combination patterns.

Section 2 utilizes six sticking patterns in an 8th-note-triplet format: Alternate Sticking, Double Paradiddle, RLL, LRR, RRL, and LLR. Each part is summarized with a series of two-bar combination patterns. Part 7 utilizes mixed-triplet stickings in two-bar combination patterns.

The four cross-sticking maneuvers, combined with the nine varied sticking patterns, offer hundreds of possibilities. Practicing them will greatly improve your cross-sticking technique, as well as your overall ability to move around the drumset with greater facility.

HOW TO PRACTICE THIS BOOK

1) Practice each exercise *slowly* at first. Increase the tempo only after each exercise can be played smoothly and accurately.
2) *Repeat* each exercise fifteen to twenty times before progressing to the next one.
3) Do not move on to the next exercise until the previous one has been *mastered*.
4) Though not notated, the bass drum should be played on beats 1, 2, 3, and 4 of every measure.
5) Practice with a metronome or drum machine, increasing the tempo *gradually* as your fluency with each exercise increases.
6) The guidance of a qualified instructor is always recommended.

The following abbreviations are used throughout this book:
SD = Snare Drum   **ST** = Small Tom   **FT** = Floor Tom

SECTION 1

PART 1: 8TH-NOTE PATTERNS USING ALTERNATE STICKING

Snare Drum To Floor Tom With Left Hand Crossing Over Right

Snare Drum To Floor Tom (Left Hand Crossing Over Right)
With Small Tom Added

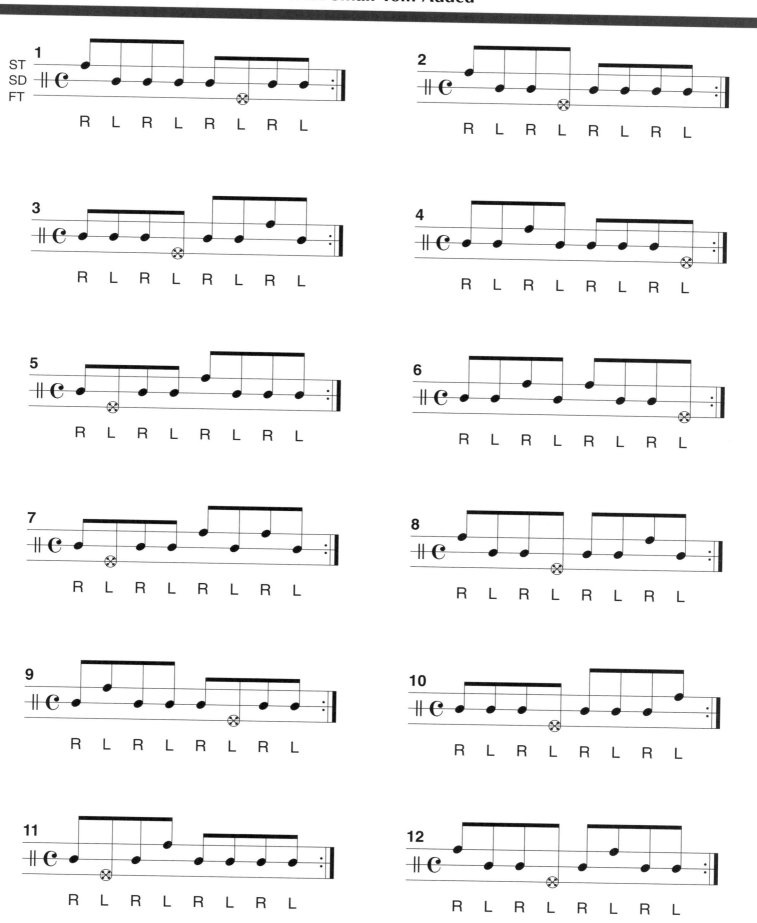

Floor Tom To Snare Drum With Right Hand Crossing Over Left

Floor Tom To Snare Drum (Right Hand Crossing Over Left)
With Small Tom Added

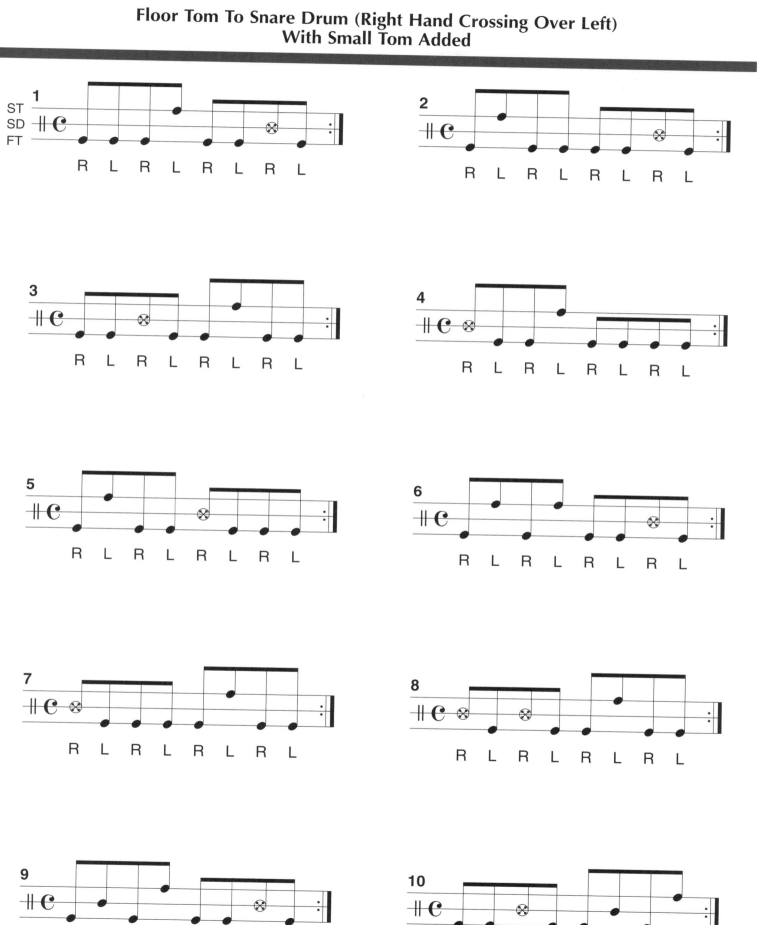

Small Tom To Floor Tom With Left Hand Crossing Over Right

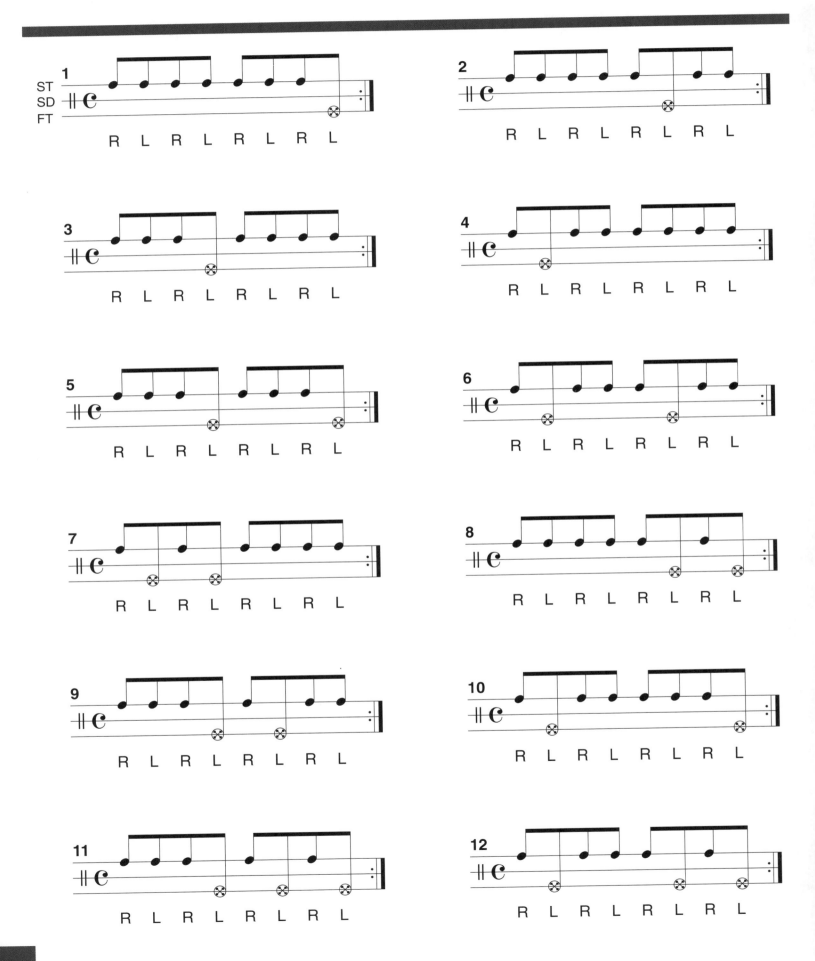

Small Tom To Floor Tom (Left Hand Crossing Over Right)
With Snare Drum Added

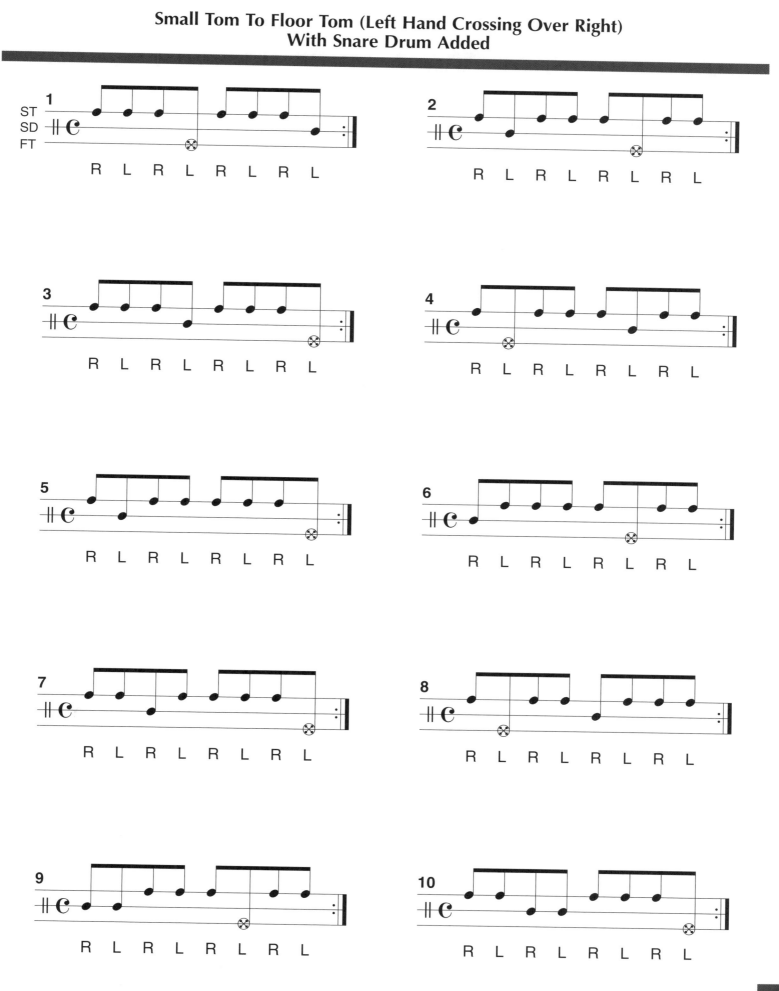

Floor Tom To Small Tom With Right Hand Crossing Over Left

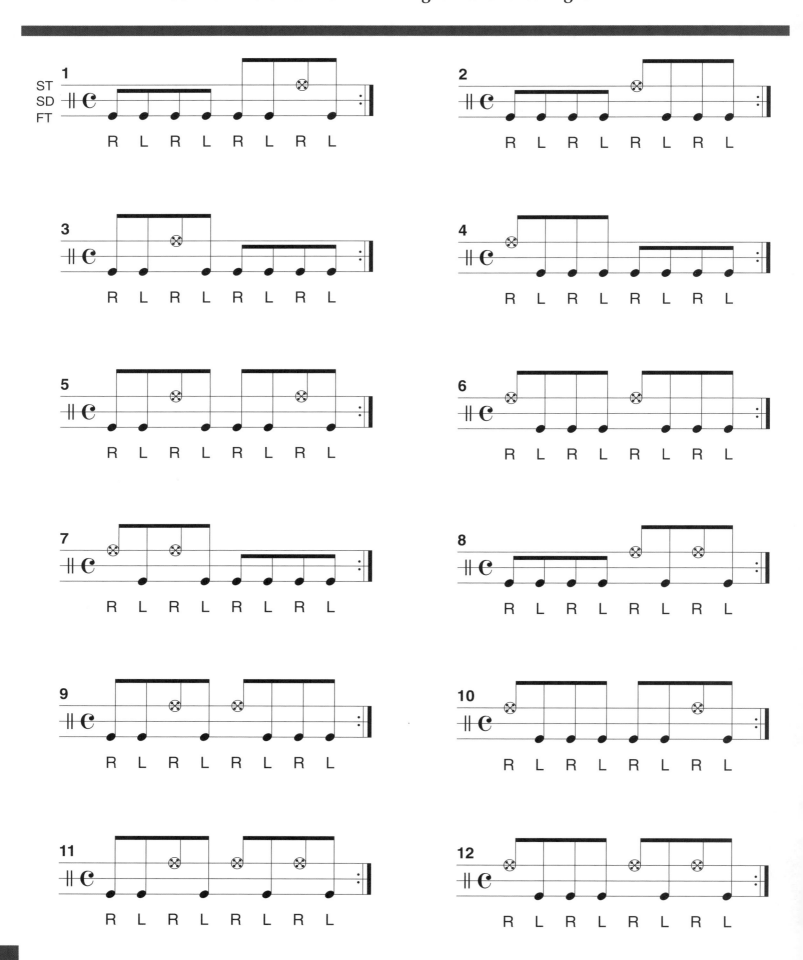

Floor Tom To Small Tom (Right Hand Crossing Over Left)
With Snare Drum Added

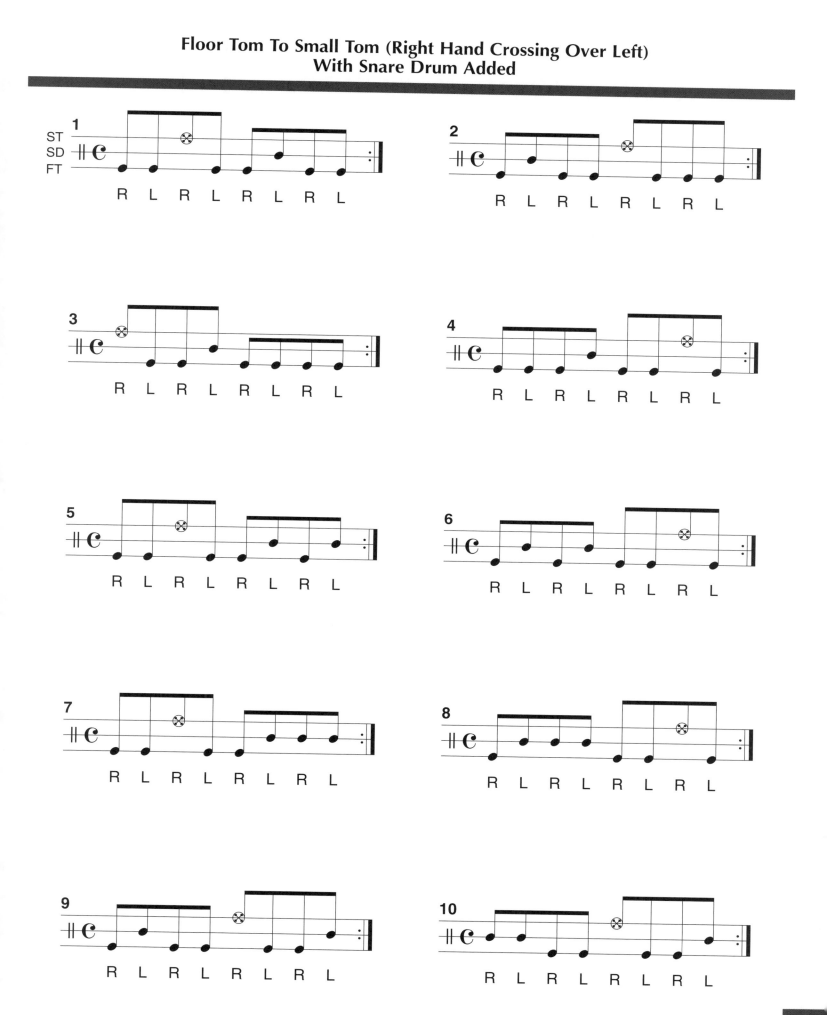

Two-Bar Combinations

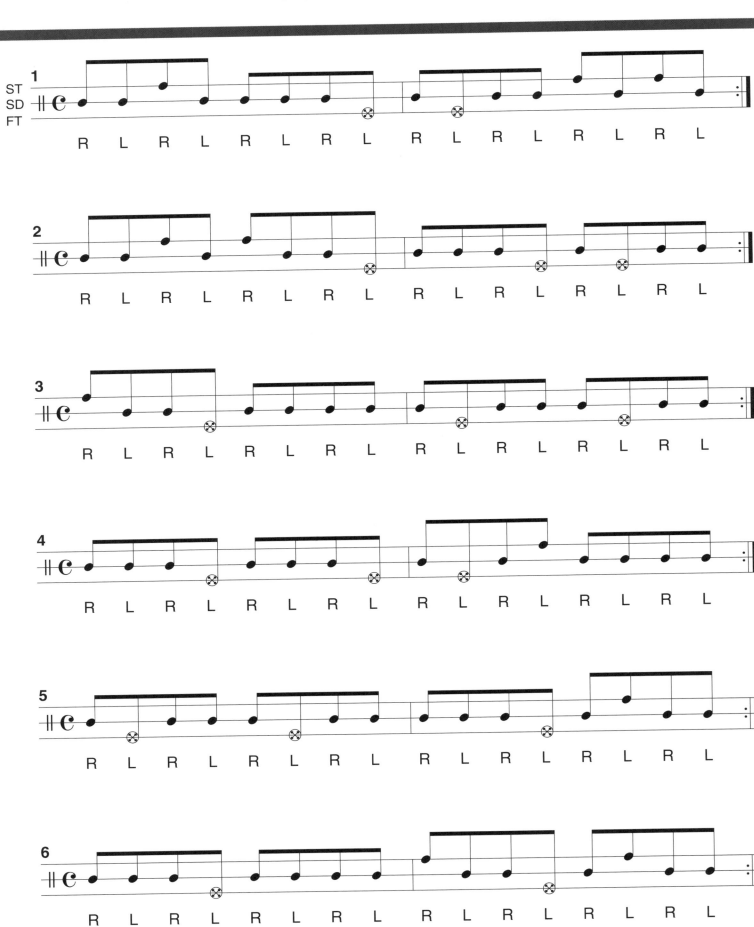

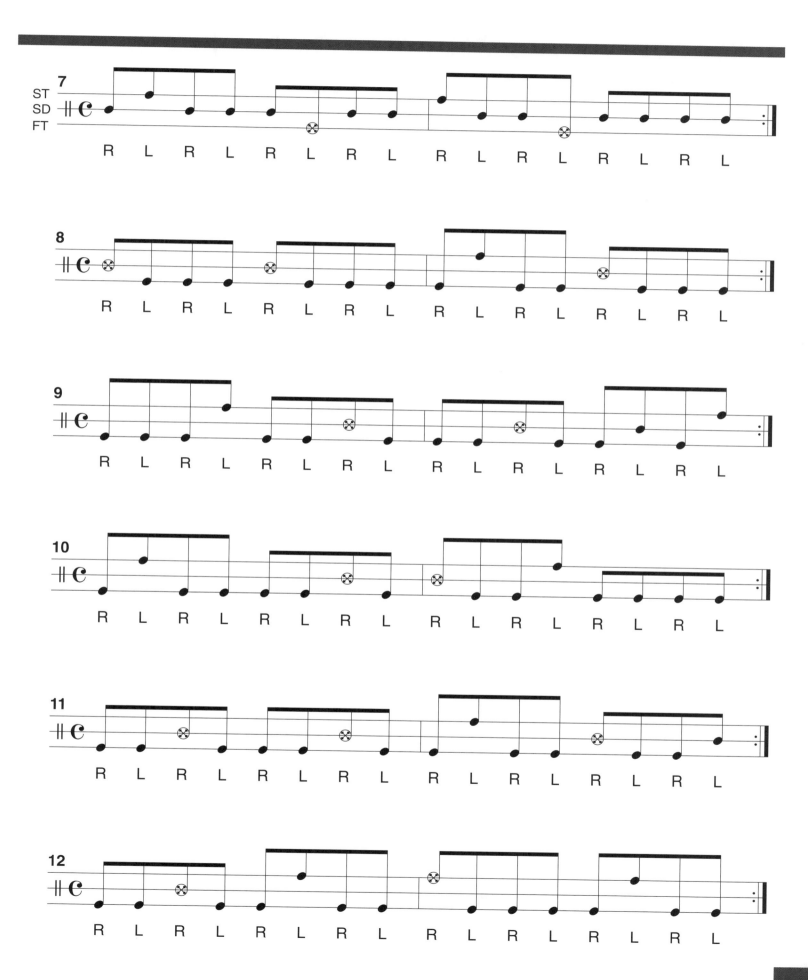

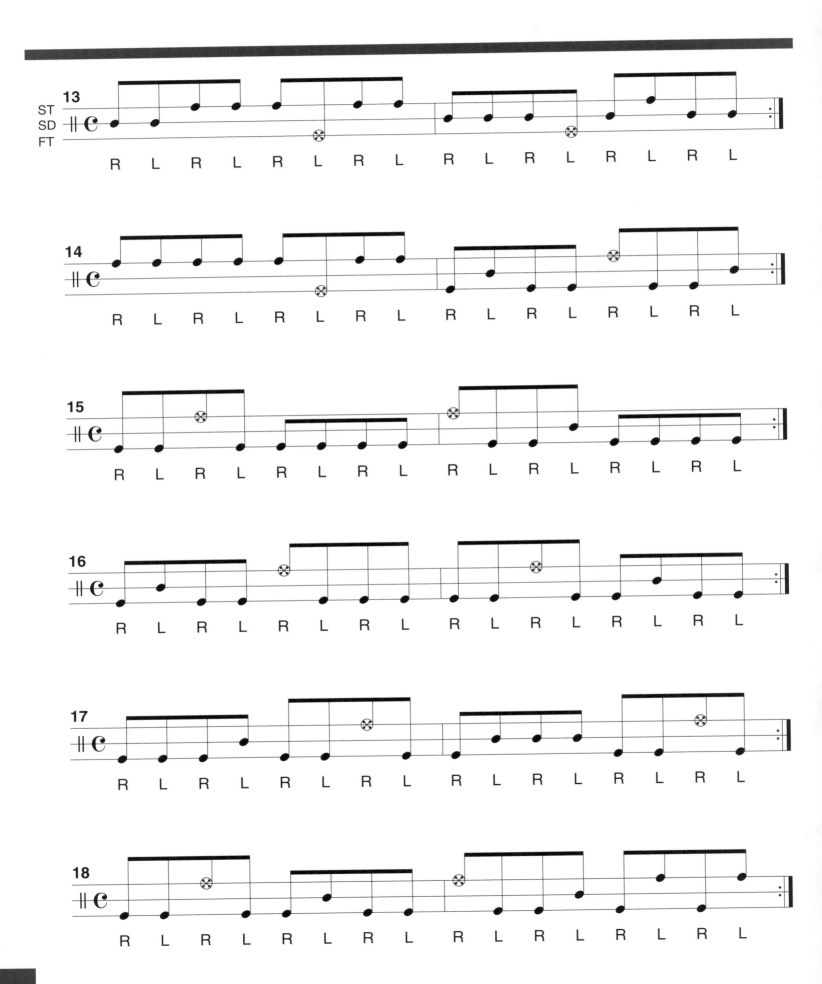

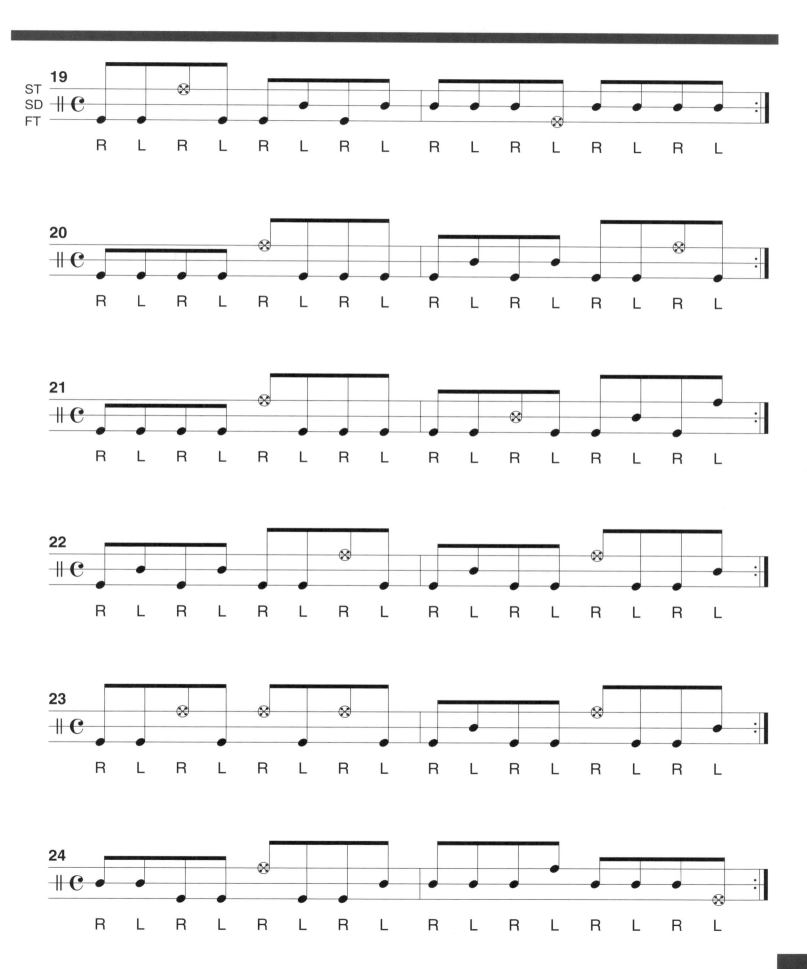

PART 2: 16TH-NOTE PATTERNS USING DOUBLE STICKING

Snare Drum To Floor Tom With Left Hand Crossing Over Right

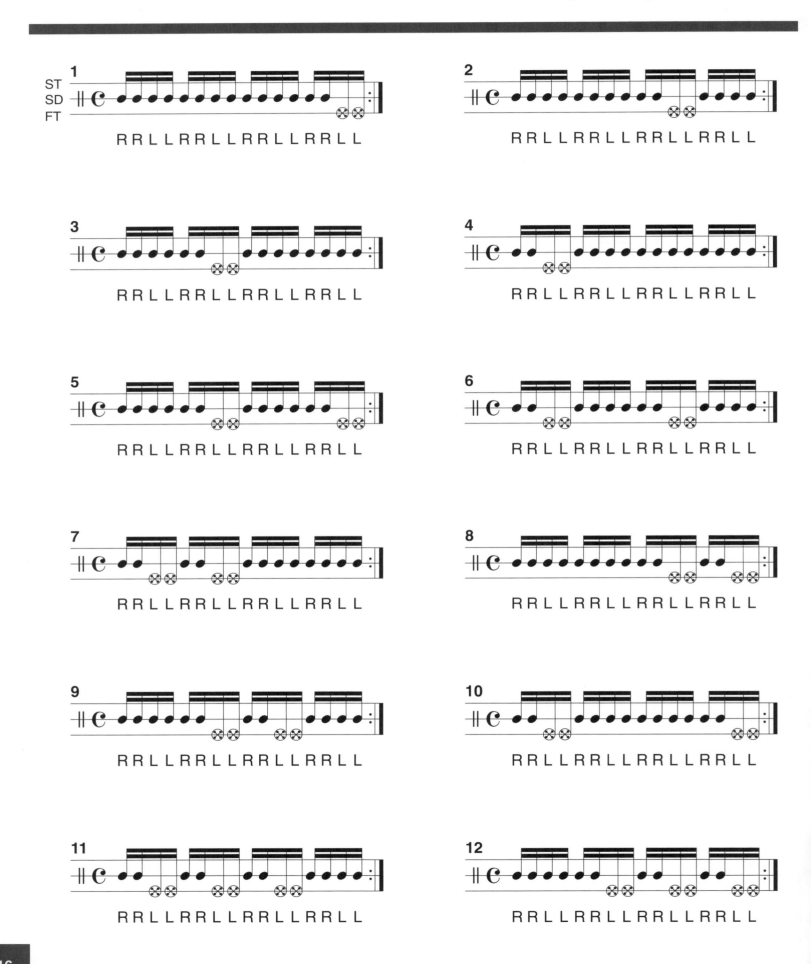

Snare Drum To Floor Tom (Left Hand Crossing Over Right)
With Small Tom Added

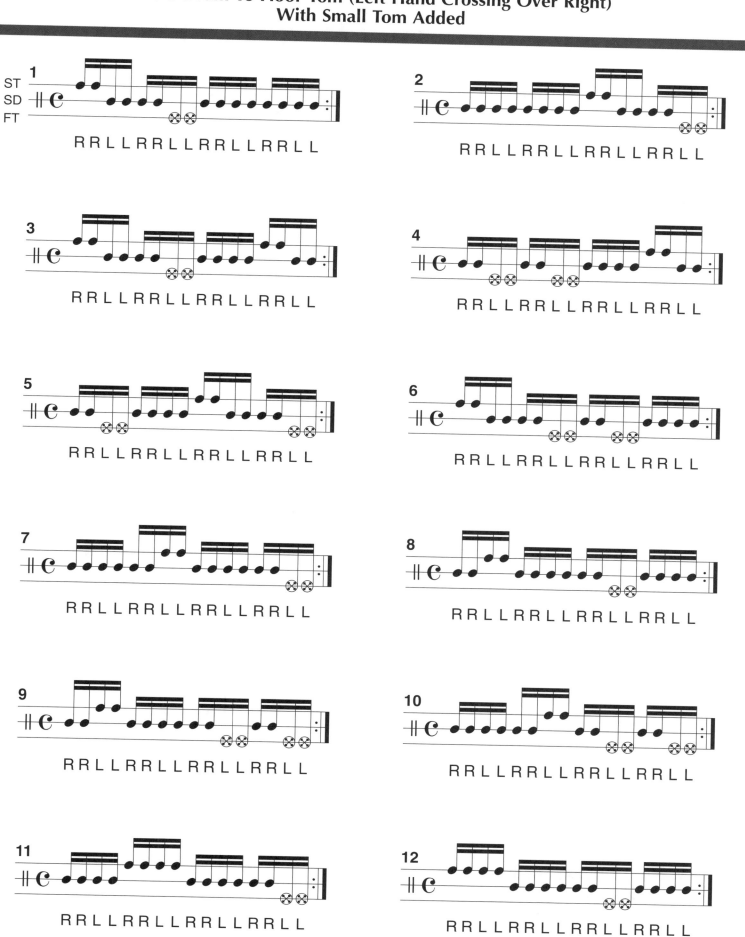

Floor Tom To Snare Drum With Right Hand Crossing Over Left

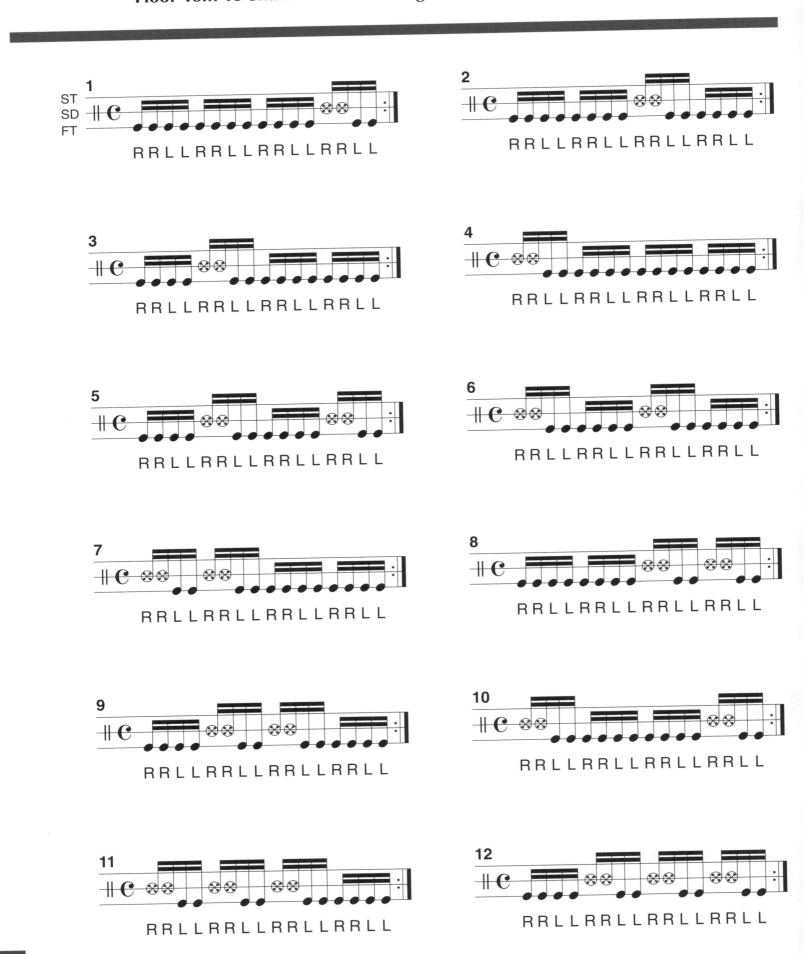

Floor Tom To Snare Drum (Right Hand Crossing Over Left)
With Small Tom Added

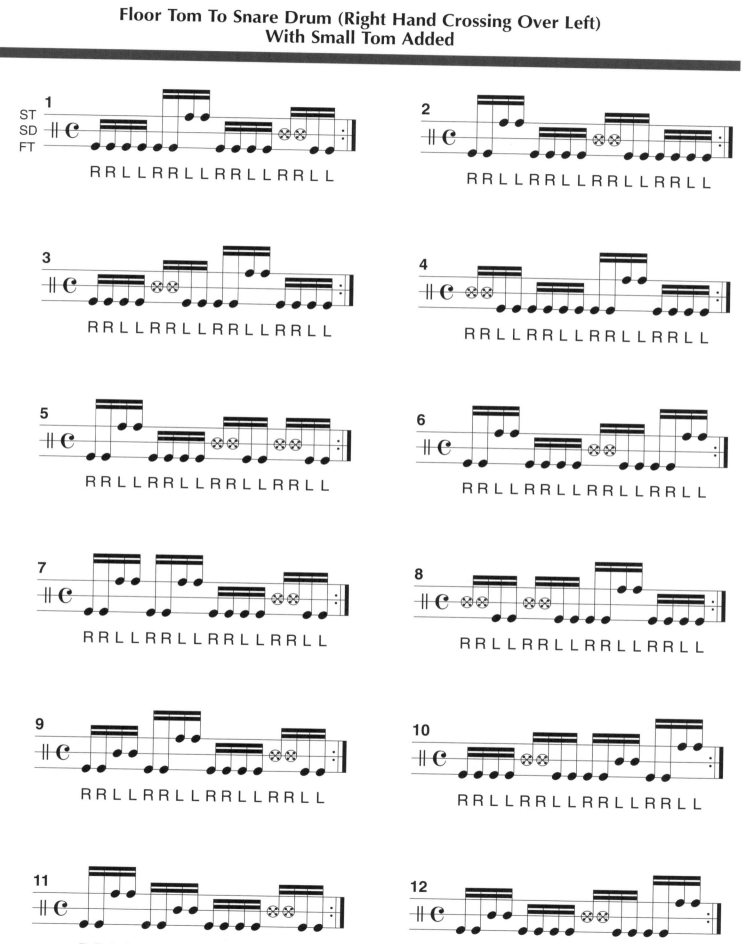

Small Tom To Floor Tom With Left Hand Crossing Over Right

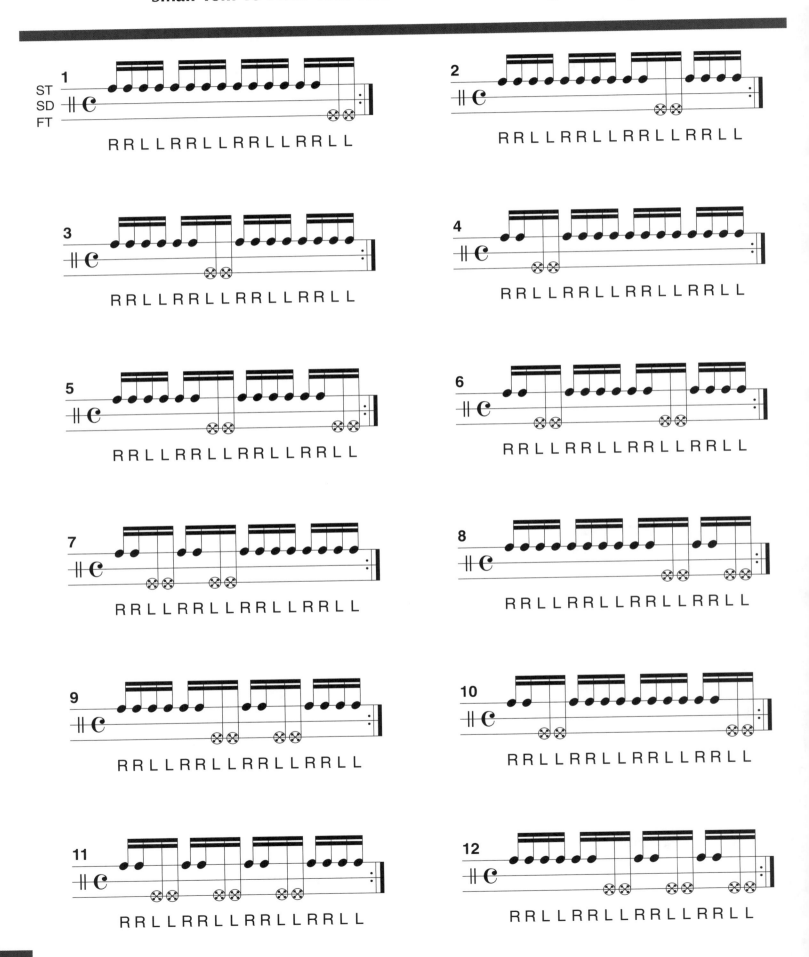

Small Tom To Floor Tom (Left Hand Crossing Over Right)
With Snare Drum Added

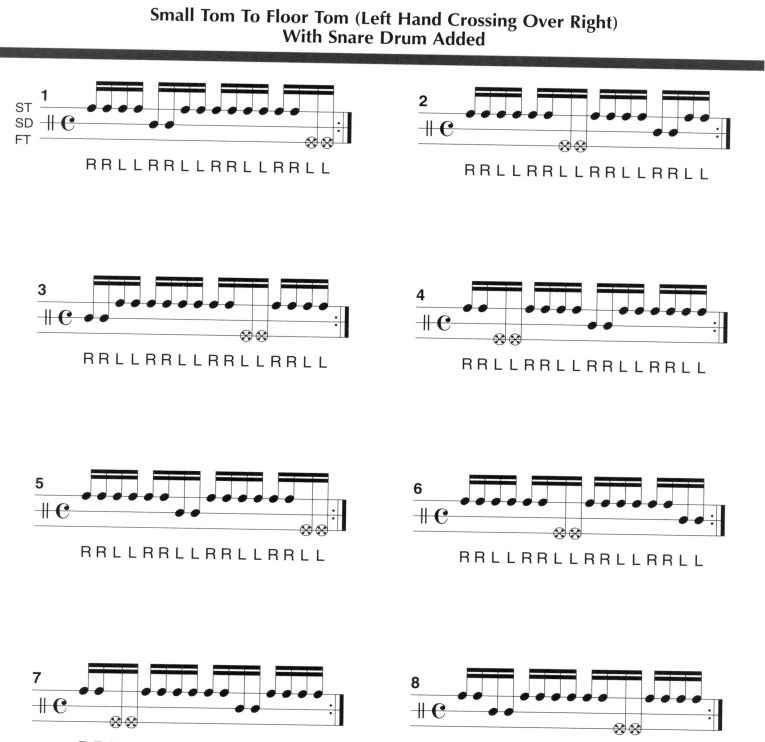

1
ST
SD
FT

R R L L R R L L R R L L R R L L

2

R R L L R R L L R R L L R R L L

3

R R L L R R L L R R L L R R L L

4

R R L L R R L L R R L L R R L L

5

R R L L R R L L R R L L R R L L

6

R R L L R R L L R R L L R R L L

7

R R L L R R L L R R L L R R L L

8

R R L L R R L L R R L L R R L L

9

R R L L R R L L R R L L R R L L

10

R R L L R R L L R R L L R R L L

Floor Tom To Small Tom With Right Hand Crossing Over Left

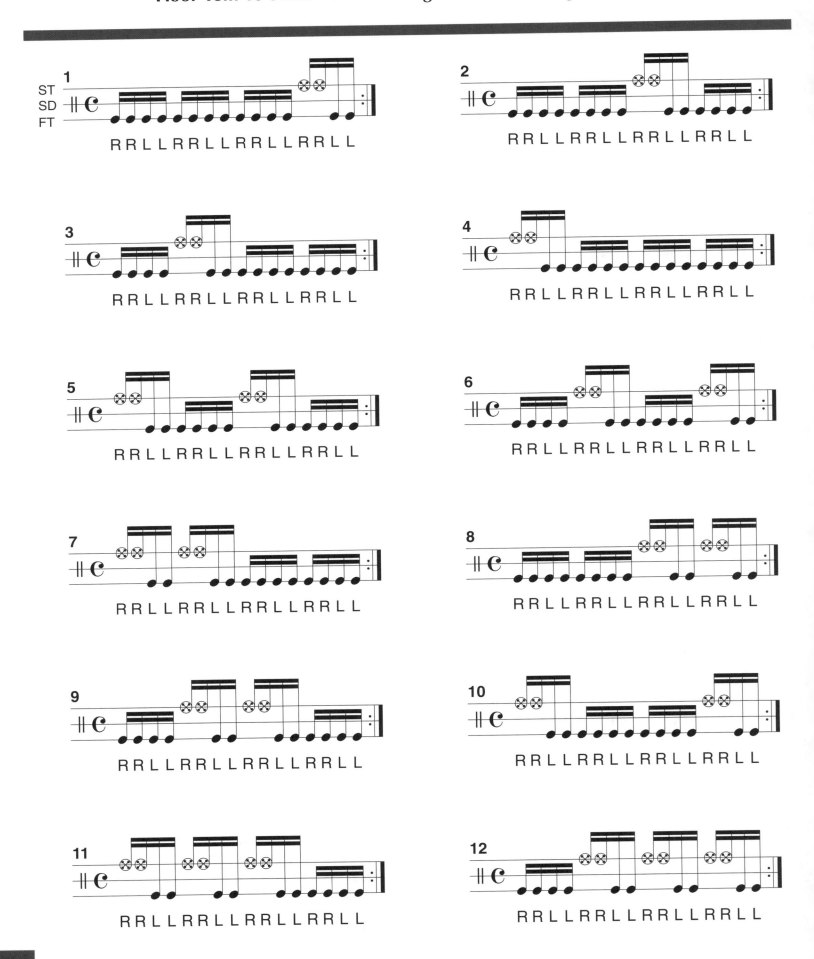

Floor Tom To Small Tom (Right Hand Crossing Over Left)
With Snare Drum Added

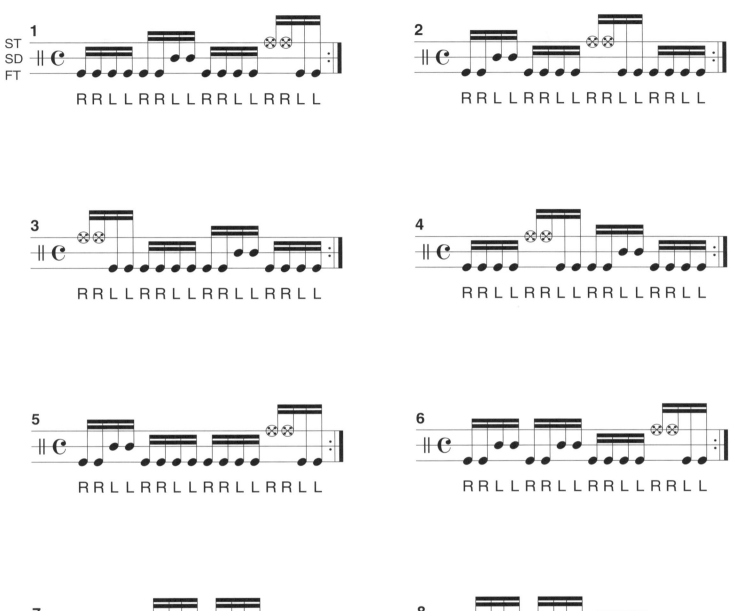

1

RRLLRRLLRRLLRRLL

2

RRLLRRLLRRLLRRLL

3

RRLLRRLLRRLLRRLL

4

RRLLRRLLRRLLRRLL

5

RRLLRRLLRRLLRRLL

6

RRLLRRLLRRLLRRLL

7

RRLLRRLLRRLLRRLL

8

RRLLRRLLRRLLRRLL

9

RRLLRRLLRRLLRRLL

10

RRLLRRLLRRLLRRLL

Two-Bar Combinations

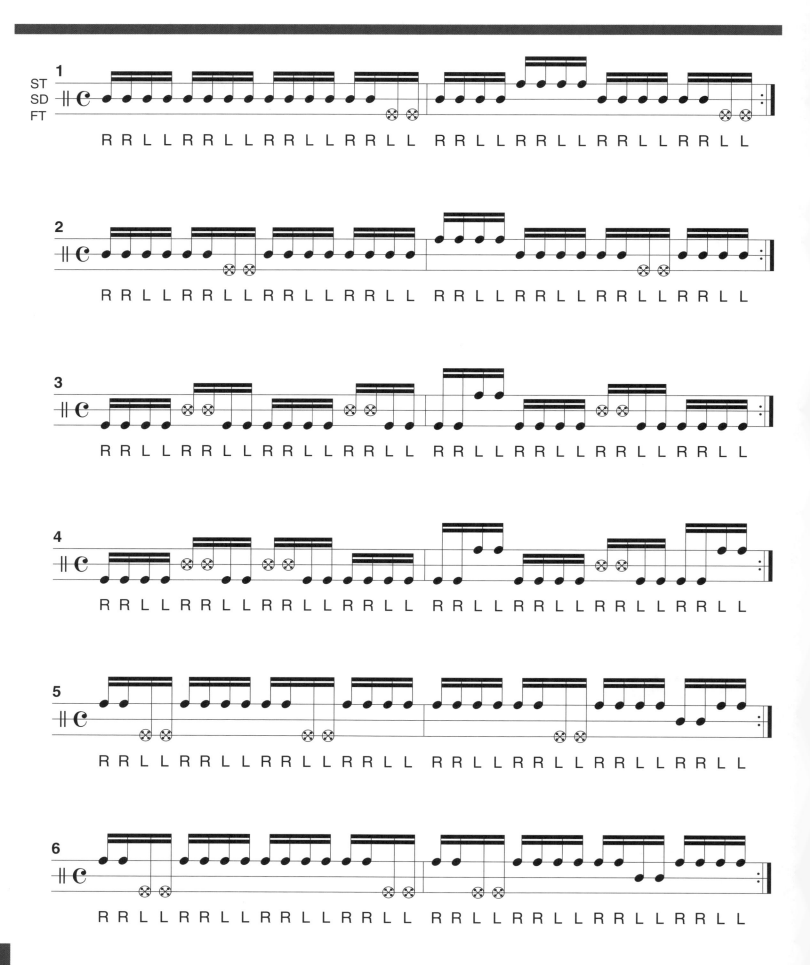

ST
SD
FT

7

R R L L R R L L R R L L R R L L R R L L R R L L R R L L R R L L

8

R R L L R R L L R R L L R R L L R R L L R R L L R R L L R R L L

9

R R L L R R L L R R L L R R L L R R L L R R L L R R L L R R L L

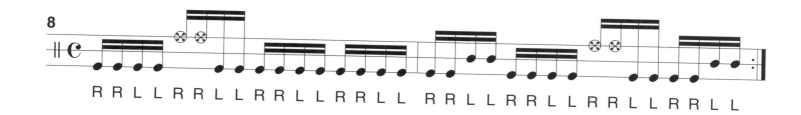

10

R R L L R R L L R R L L R R L L R R L L R R L L R R L L R R L L

11

R R L L R R L L R R L L R R L L R R L L R R L L R R L L R R L L

12

R R L L R R L L R R L L R R L L R R L L R R L L R R L L R R L L

PART 3: 16TH-NOTE PATTERNS USING PARADIDDLE STICKING

Snare Drum To Floor Tom With Left Hand Crossing Over Right

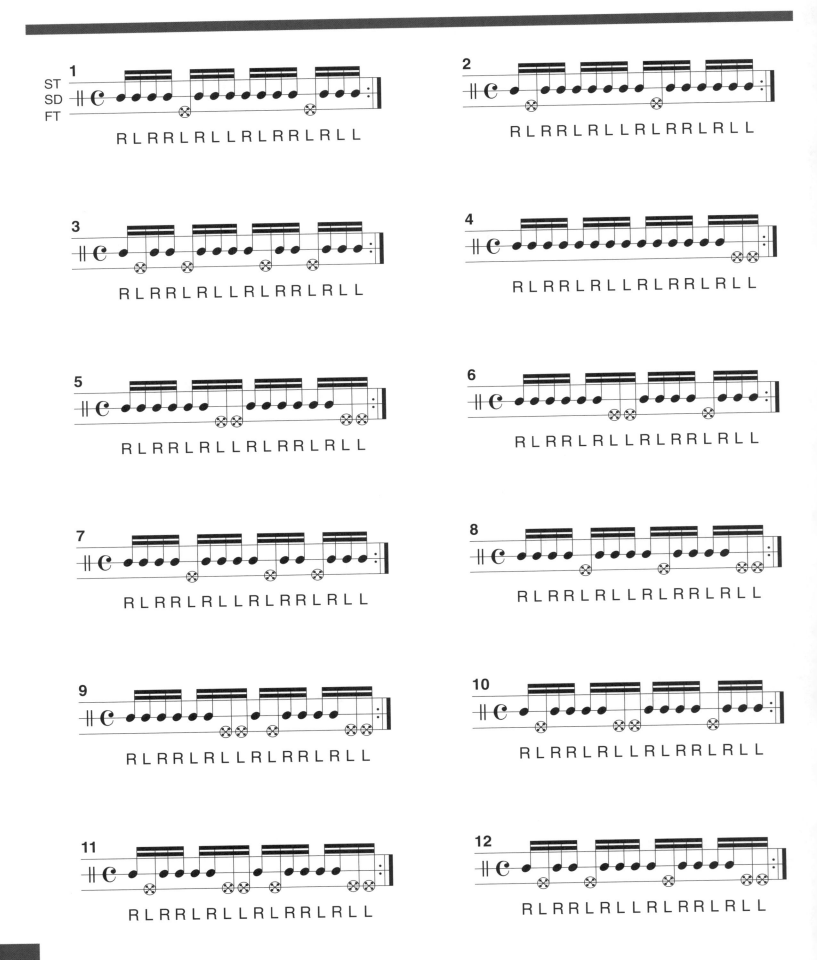

Snare Drum To Floor Tom (Left Hand Crossing Over Right)
With Small Tom Added

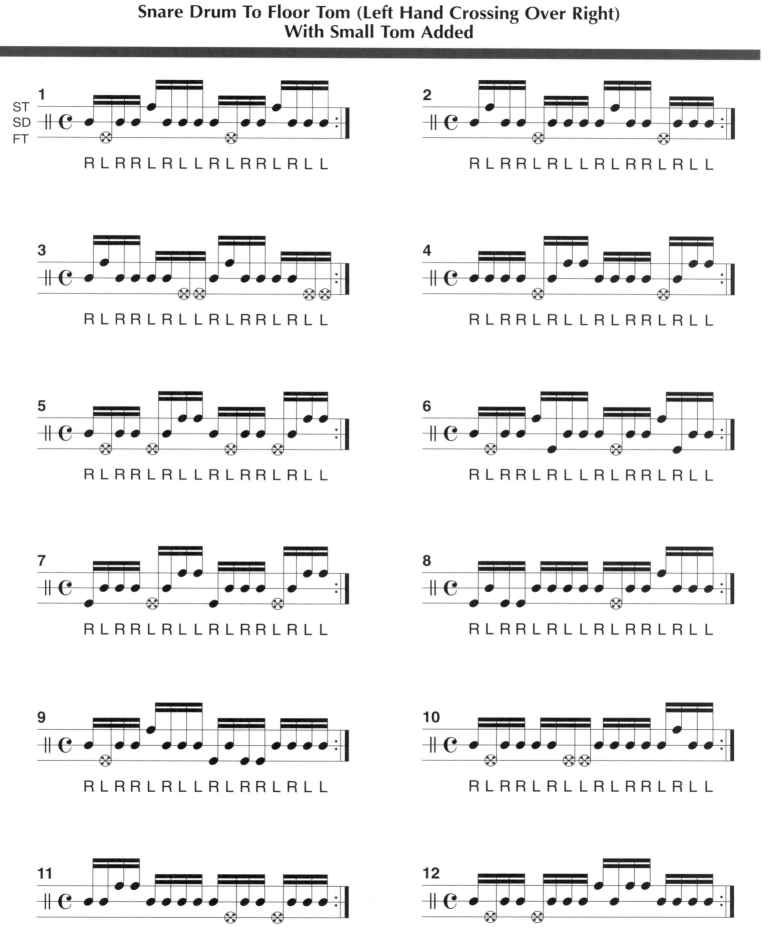

Floor Tom To Snare Drum With Right Hand Crossing Over Left

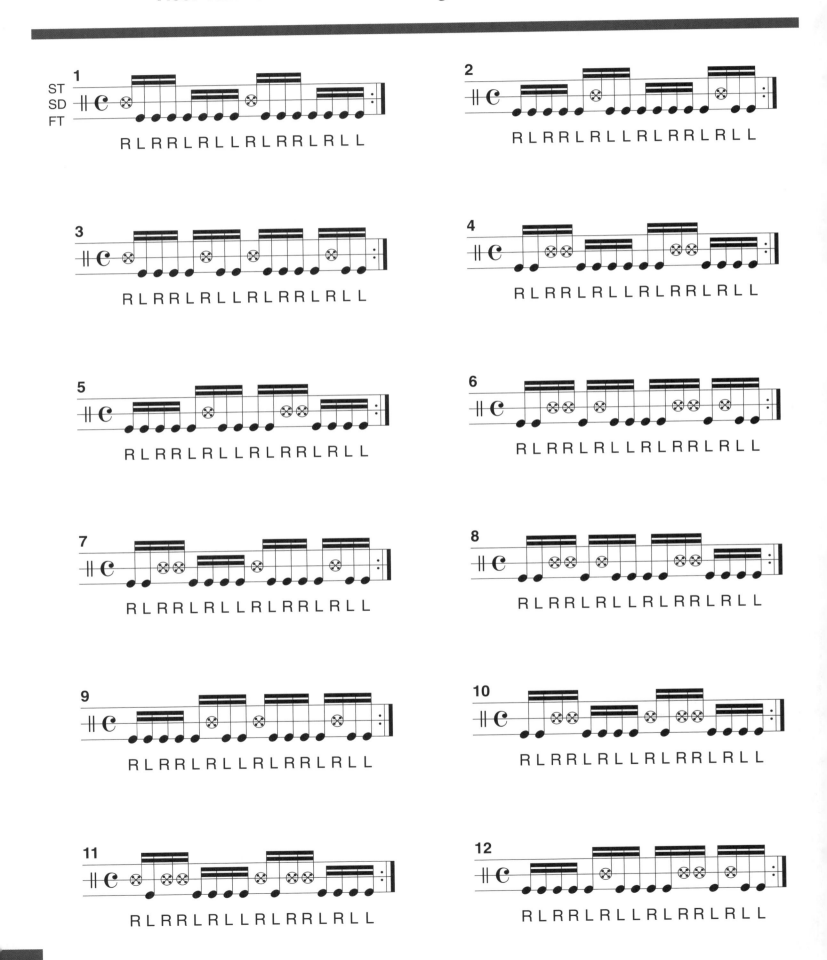

Floor Tom To Snare Drum (Right Hand Crossing Over Left)
With Small Tom Added

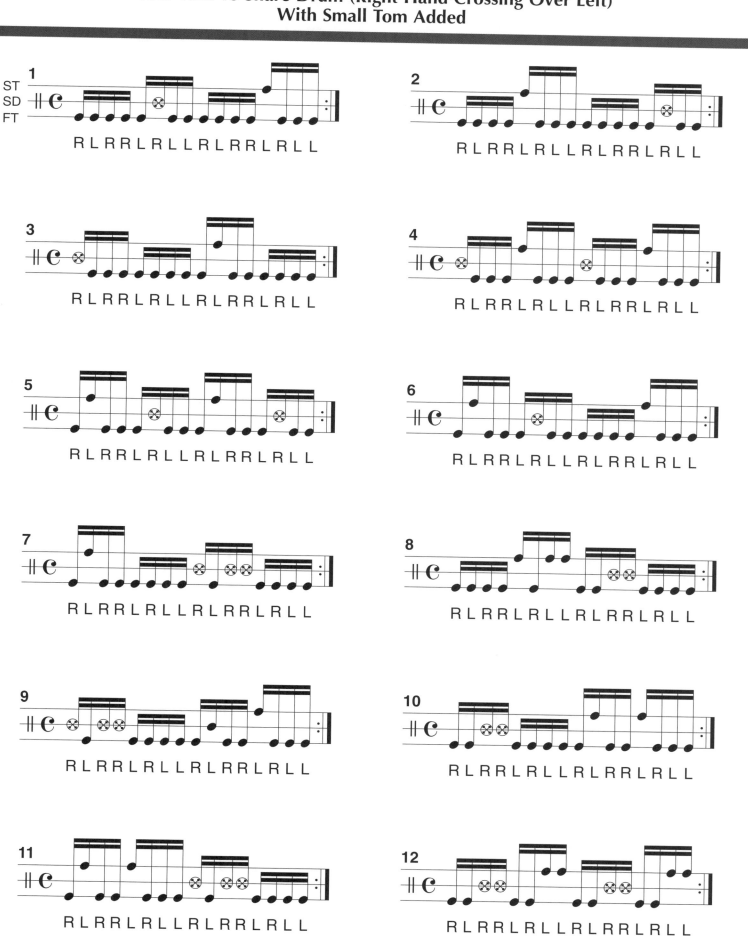

Small Tom To Floor Tom With Left Hand Crossing Over Right

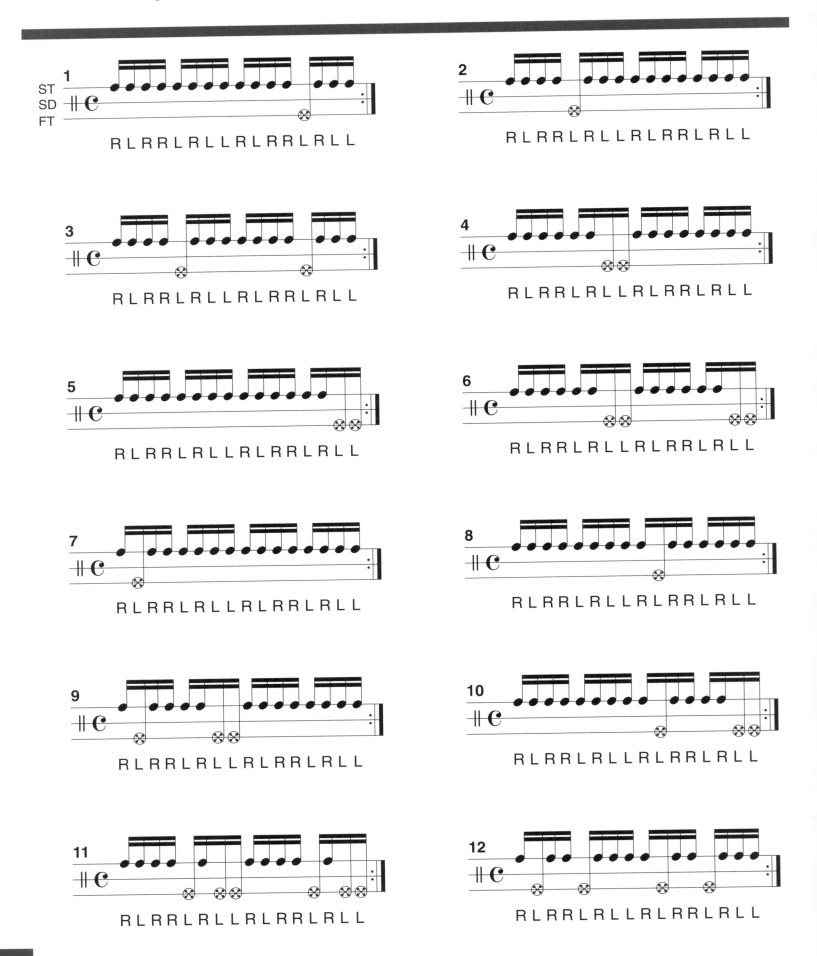

Small Tom To Floor Tom (Left Hand Crossing Over Right)
With Snare Drum Added

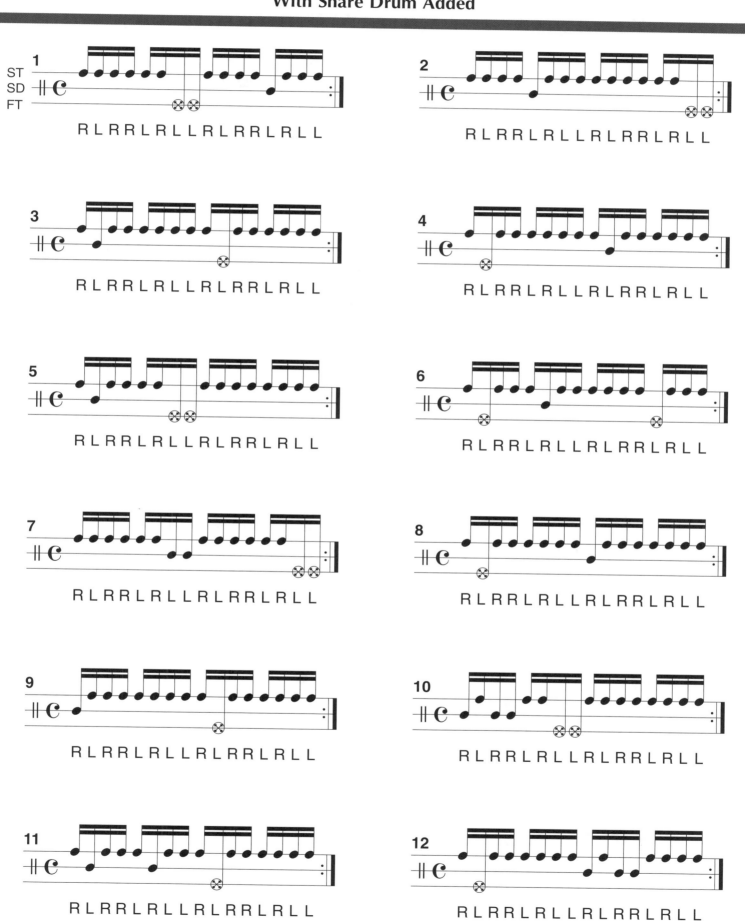

Floor Tom To Small Tom With Right Hand Crossing Over Left

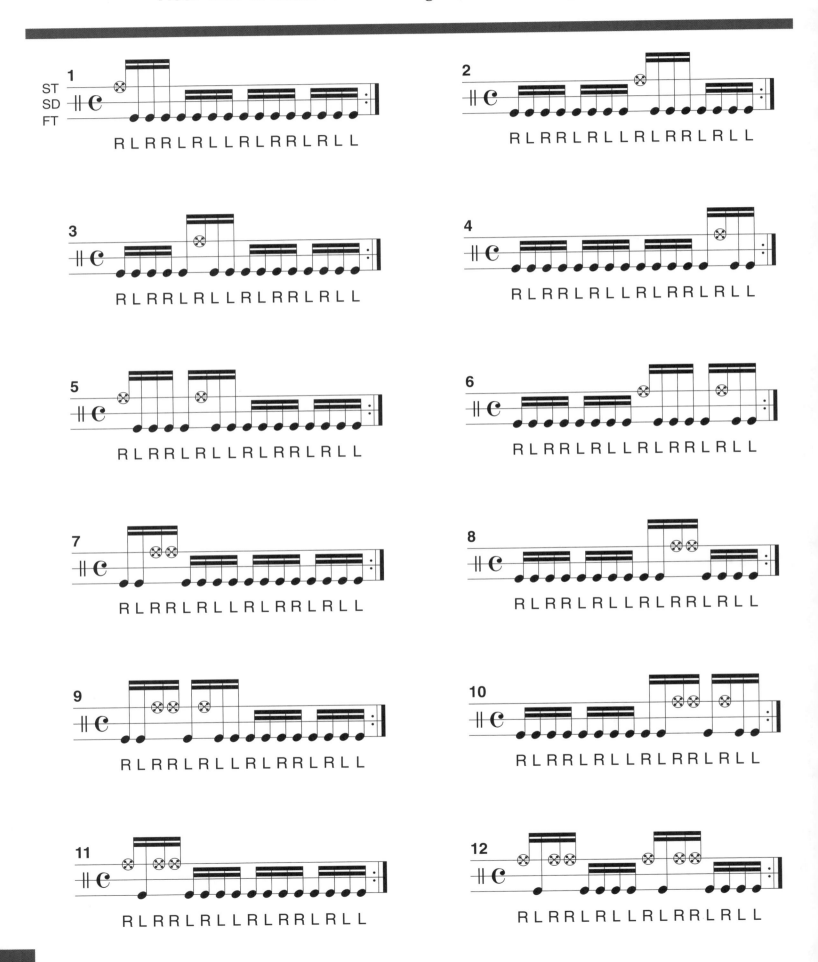

Floor Tom To Small Tom (Right Hand Crossing Over Left)
With Snare Drum Added

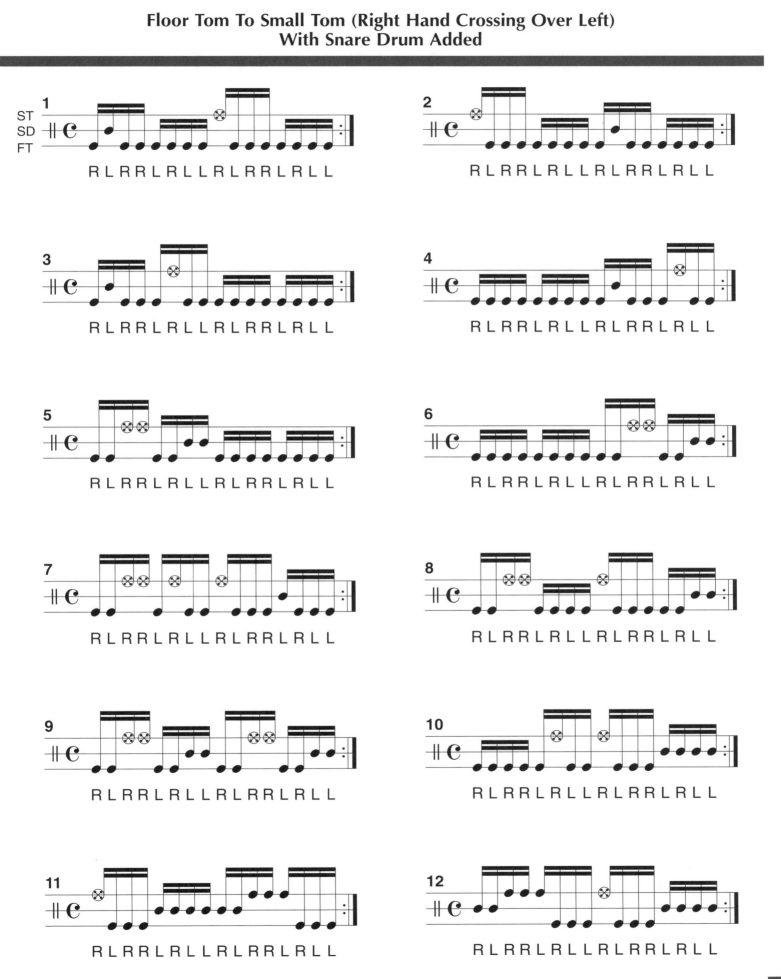

Two-Bar Combinations

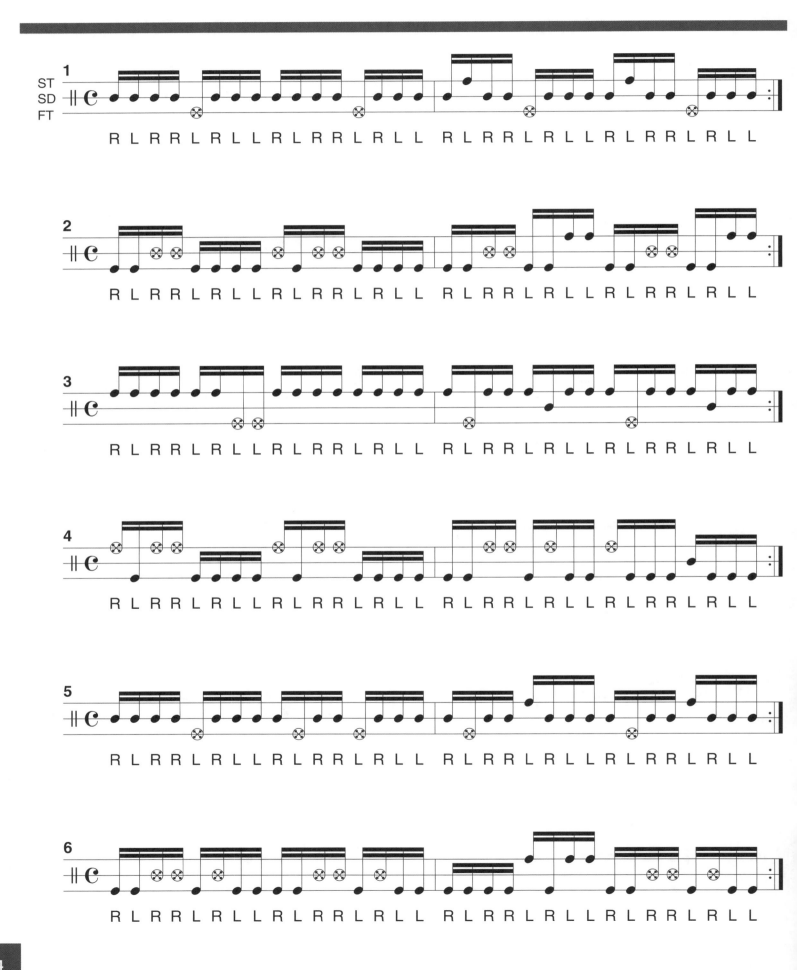

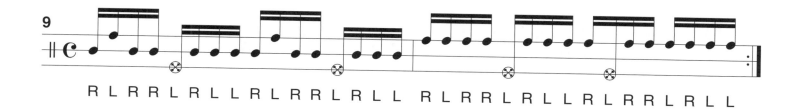

Two-Bar Combinations: Double Sticking To Paradiddles

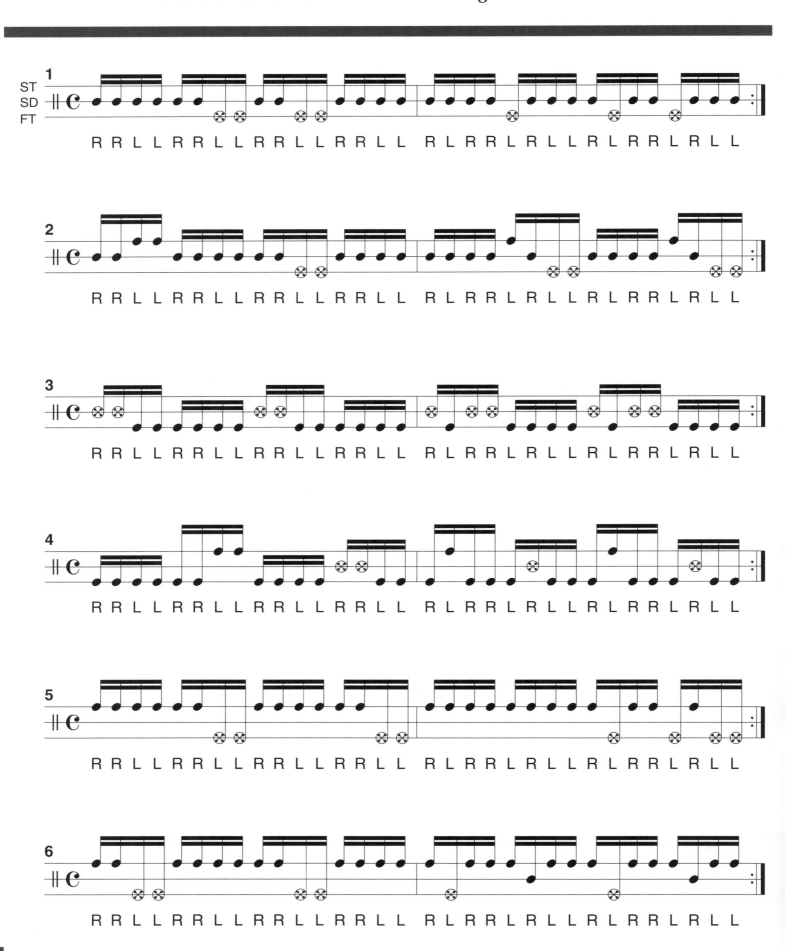

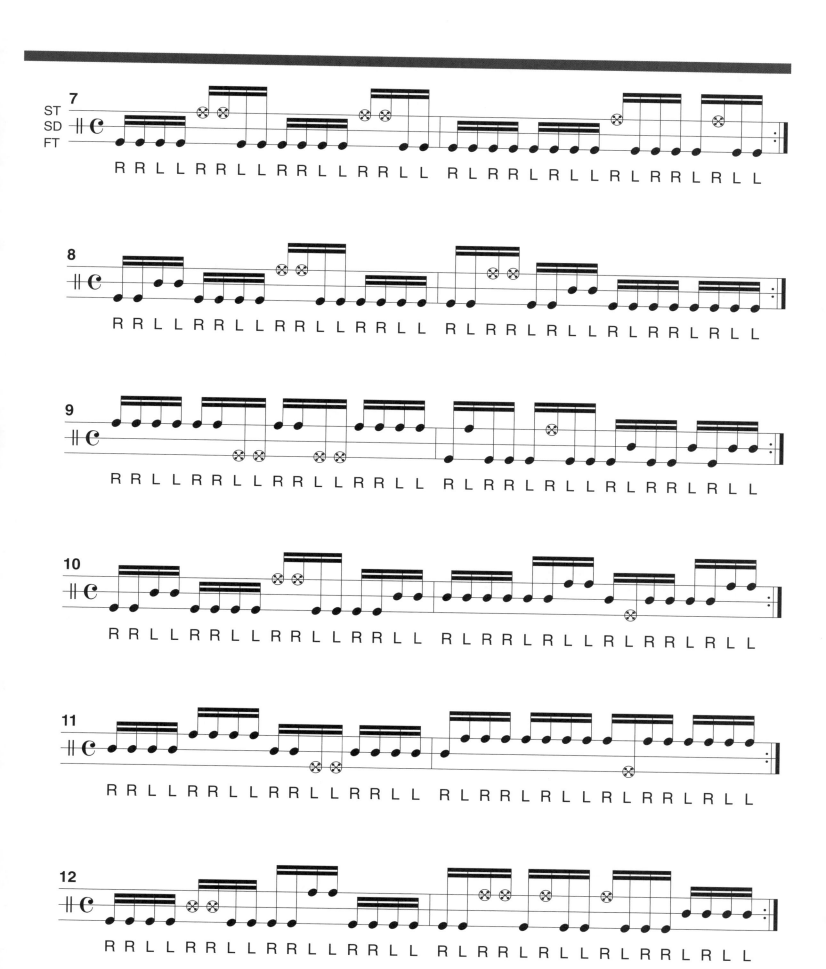

Two-Bar Combinations: Paradiddles To Double Sticking

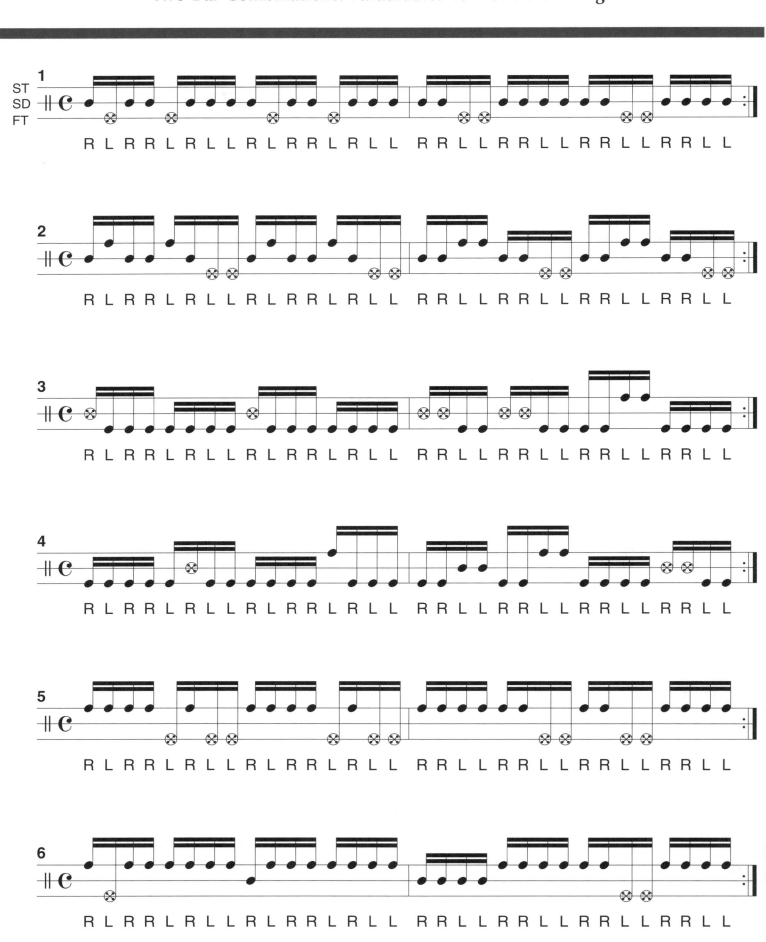

1

ST
SD
FT

R L R R L R L L R L R R L R L L R R L L R R L L R R L L R R L L

2

R L R R L R L L R L R R L R L L R R L L R R L L R R L L R R L L

3

R L R R L R L L R L R R L R L L R R L L R R L L R R L L R R L L

4

R L R R L R L L R L R R L R L L R R L L R R L L R R L L R R L L

5

R L R R L R L L R L R R L R L L R R L L R R L L R R L L R R L L

6

R L R R L R L L R L R R L R L L R R L L R R L L R R L L R R L L

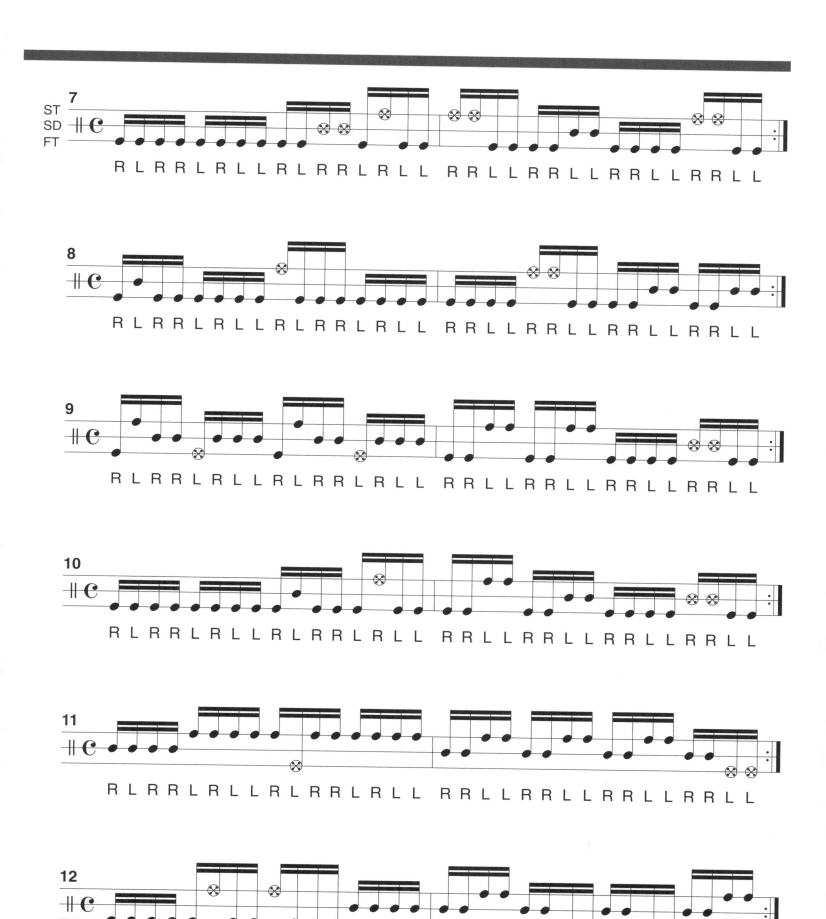

SECTION 2

PART 1: TRIPLET PATTERNS USING ALTERNATE STICKING

Snare Drum To Floor Tom With Left Hand Crossing Over Right

Remember to continue playing the bass drum on the 1, 2, 3, and 4 of every bar as you progress through the triplet section of this book. Also, be sure to play each exercise slowly at first, repeating each one fifteen to twenty times before moving on. Practice with a metronome, increasing the speed gradually.

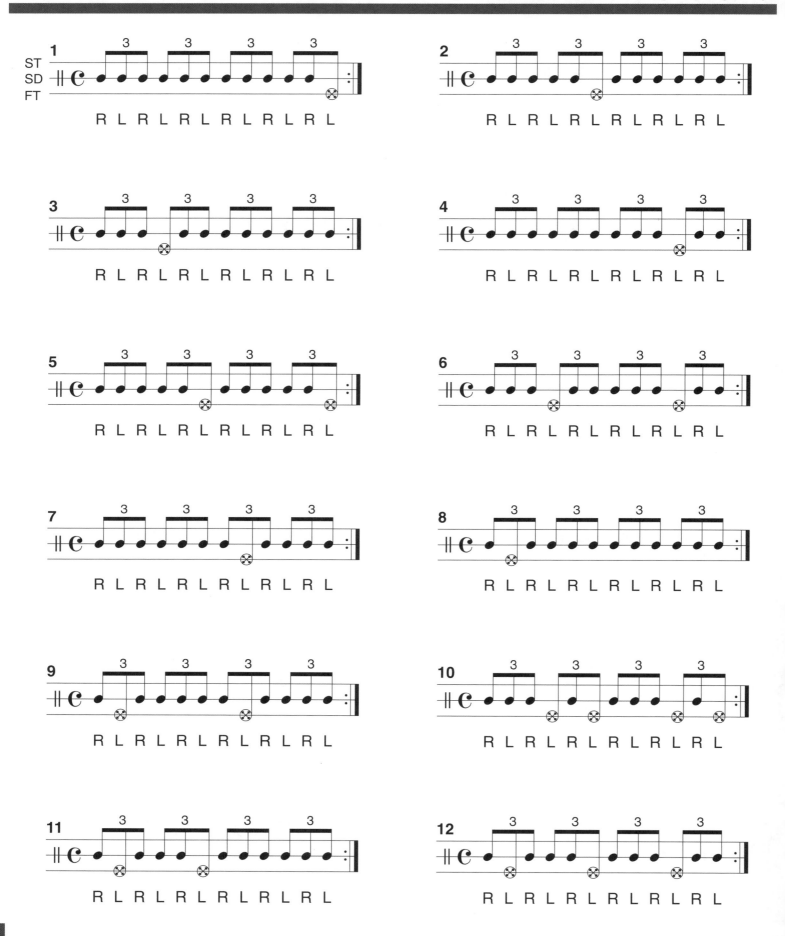

Snare Drum To Floor Tom (Left Hand Crossing Over Right)
With Small Tom Added

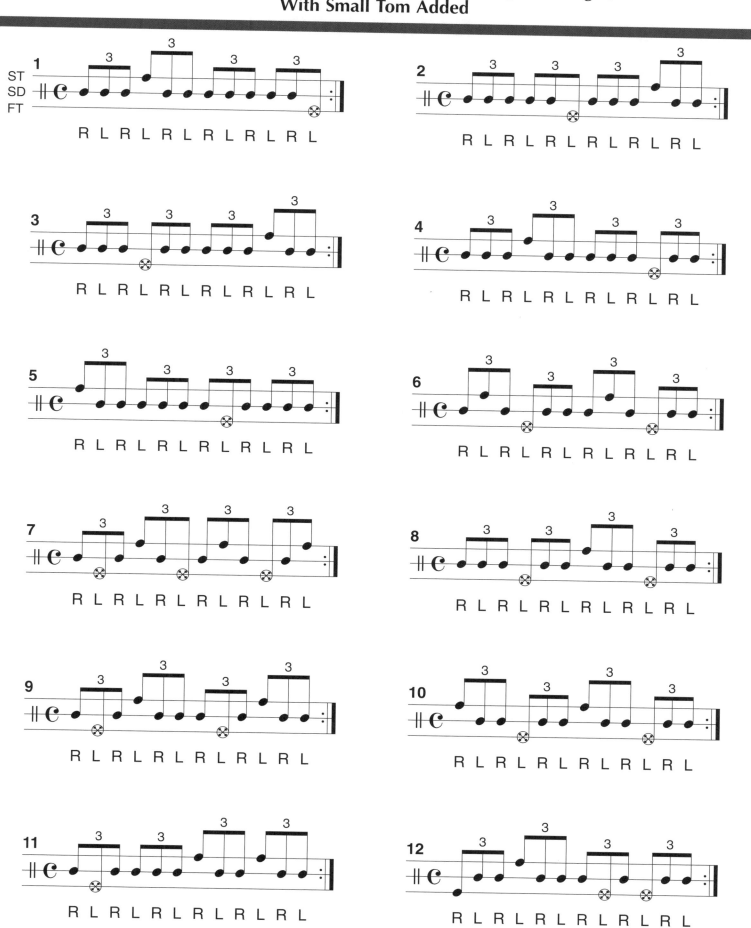

13

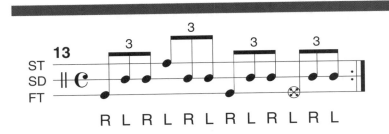

ST
SD
FT

R L R L R L R L R L R L

14

R L R L R L R L R L R L

15

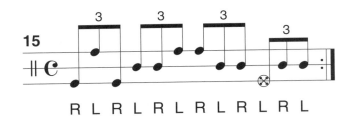

R L R L R L R L R L R L

16

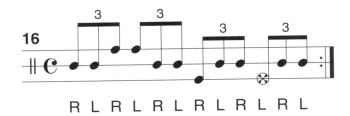

R L R L R L R L R L R L

17

R L R L R L R L R L R L

18

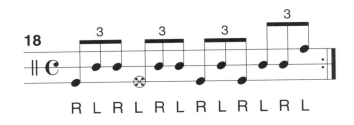

R L R L R L R L R L R L

19

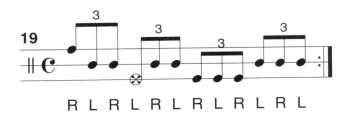

R L R L R L R L R L R L

20

R L R L R L R L R L R L

21

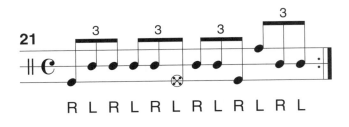

R L R L R L R L R L R L

22

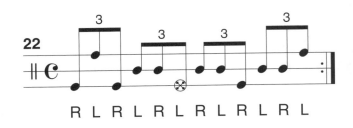

R L R L R L R L R L R L

23

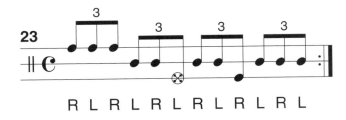

R L R L R L R L R L R L

24

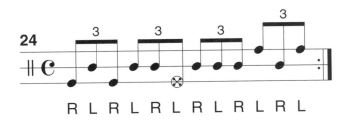

R L R L R L R L R L R L

Floor Tom To Snare Drum With Right Hand Crossing Over Left

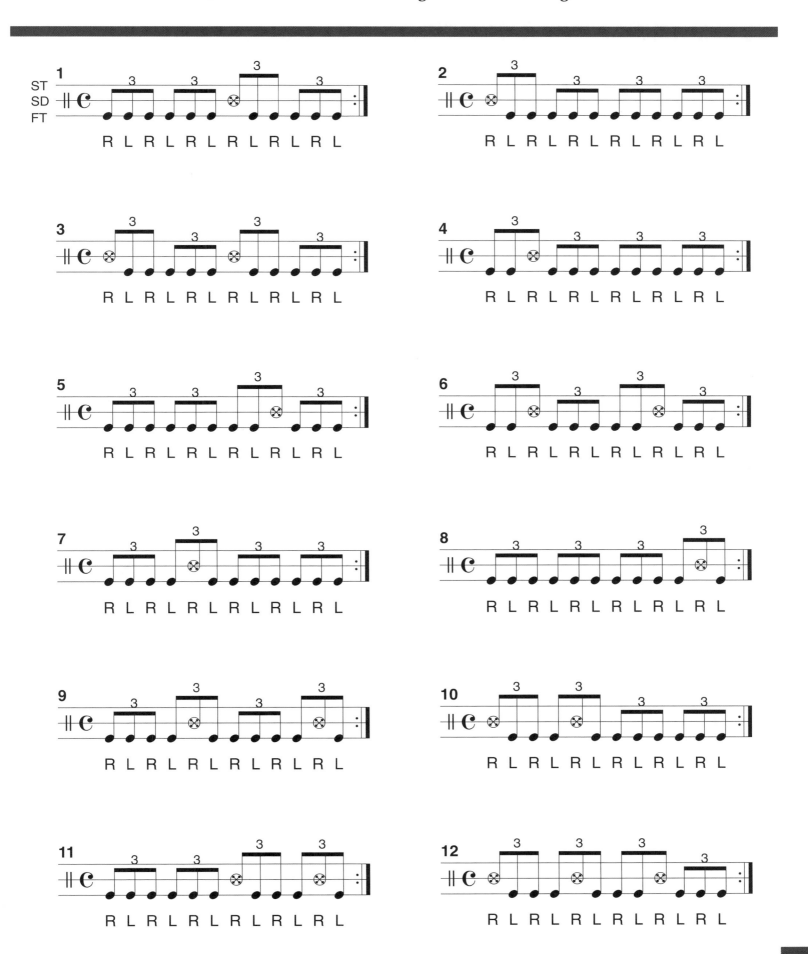

Floor Tom To Snare Drum (Right Hand Crossing Over Left)
With Small Tom Added

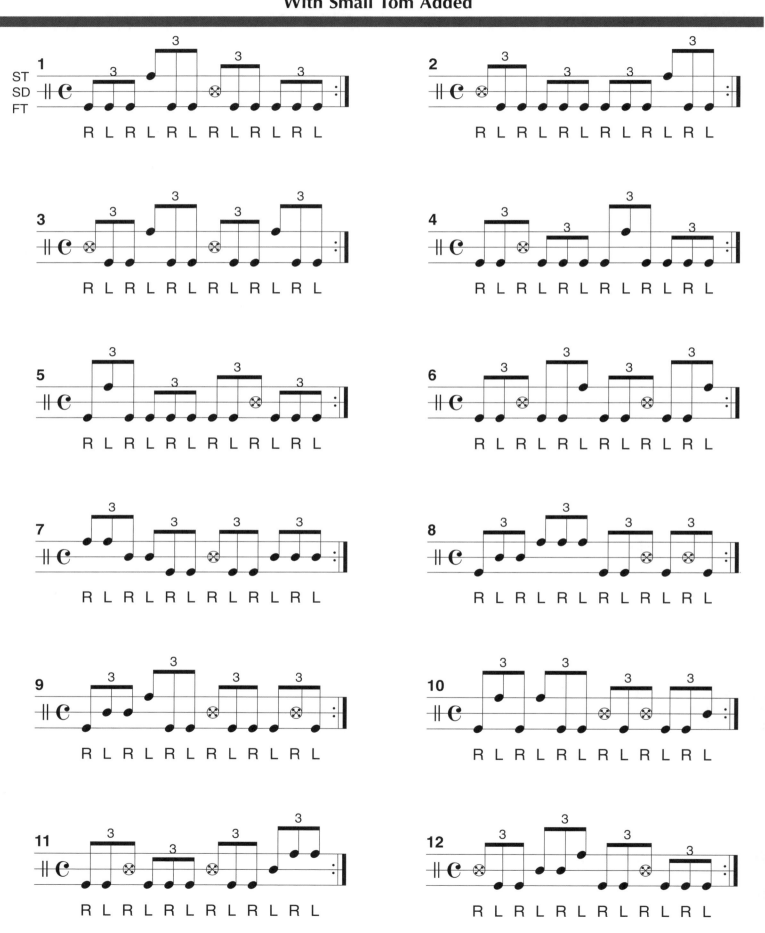

Small Tom To Floor Tom With Left Hand Crossing Over Right

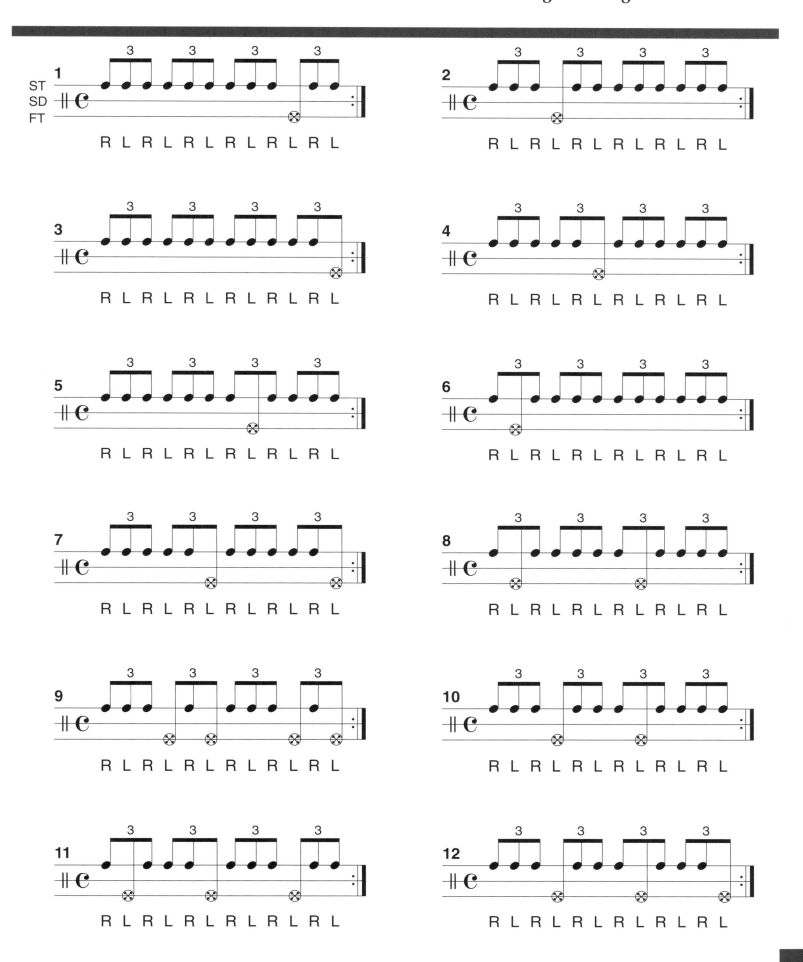

Small Tom To Floor Tom (Left Hand Crossing Over Right)
With Snare Drum Added

Floor Tom To Small Tom With Right Hand Crossing Over Left

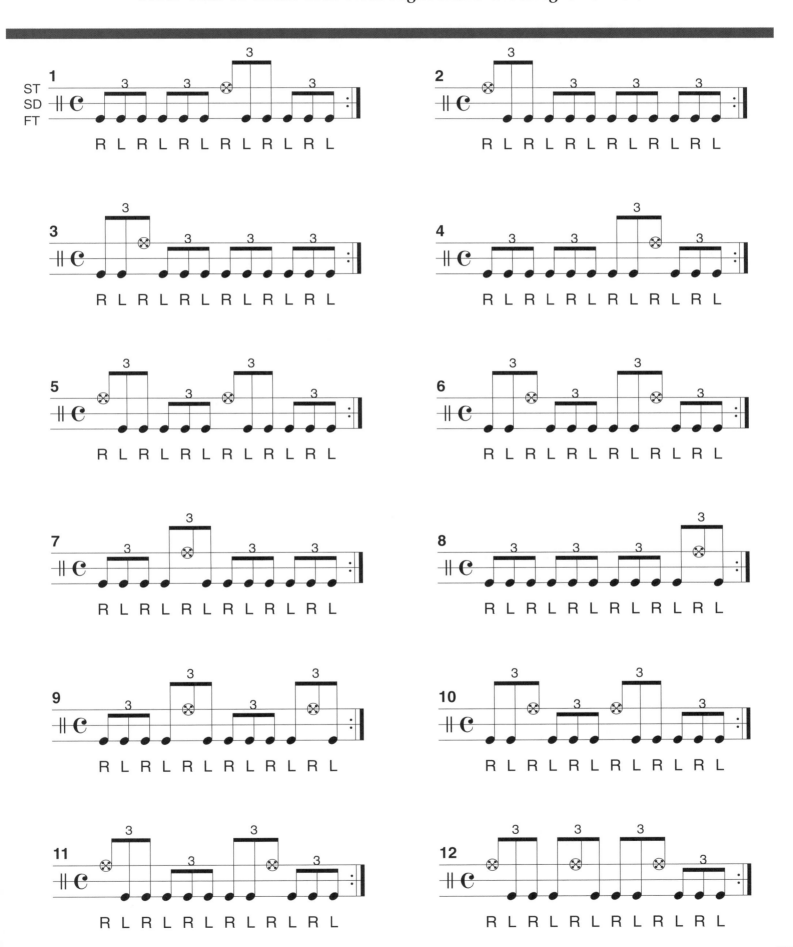

Floor Tom To Small Tom (Right Hand Crossing Over Left)
With Snare Drum Added

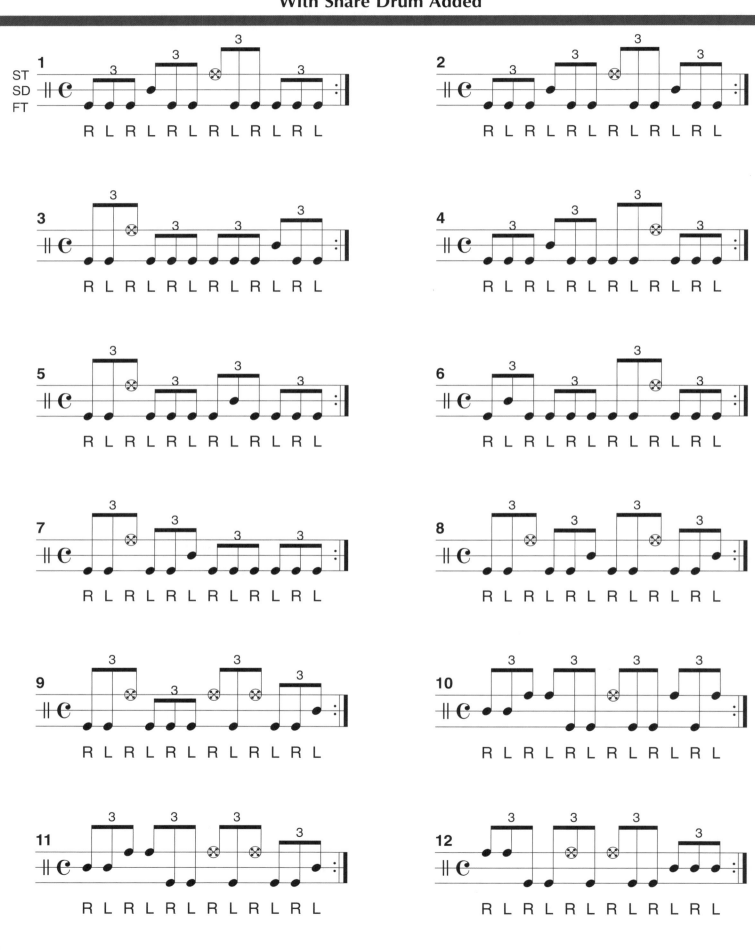

Two-Bar Combinations

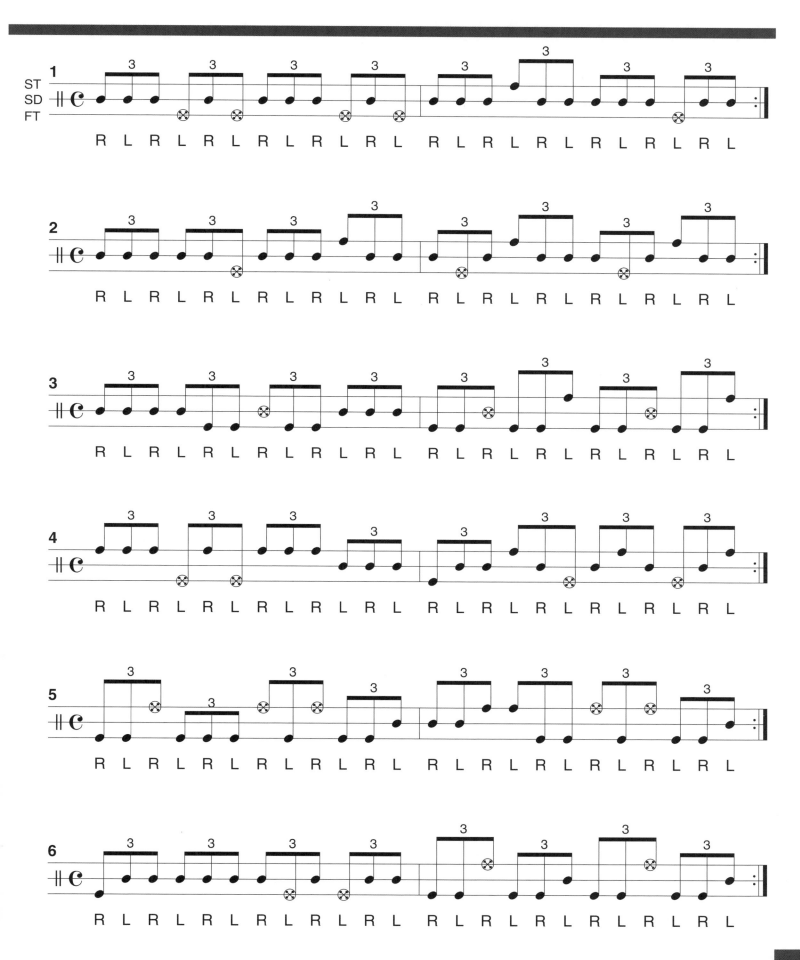

PART 2: TRIPLET PATTERNS USING DOUBLE PARADIDDLE STICKING

Snare Drum To Floor Tom With Left Hand Crossing Over Right

Snare Drum To Floor Tom (Left Hand Crossing Over Right)
With Small Tom Added

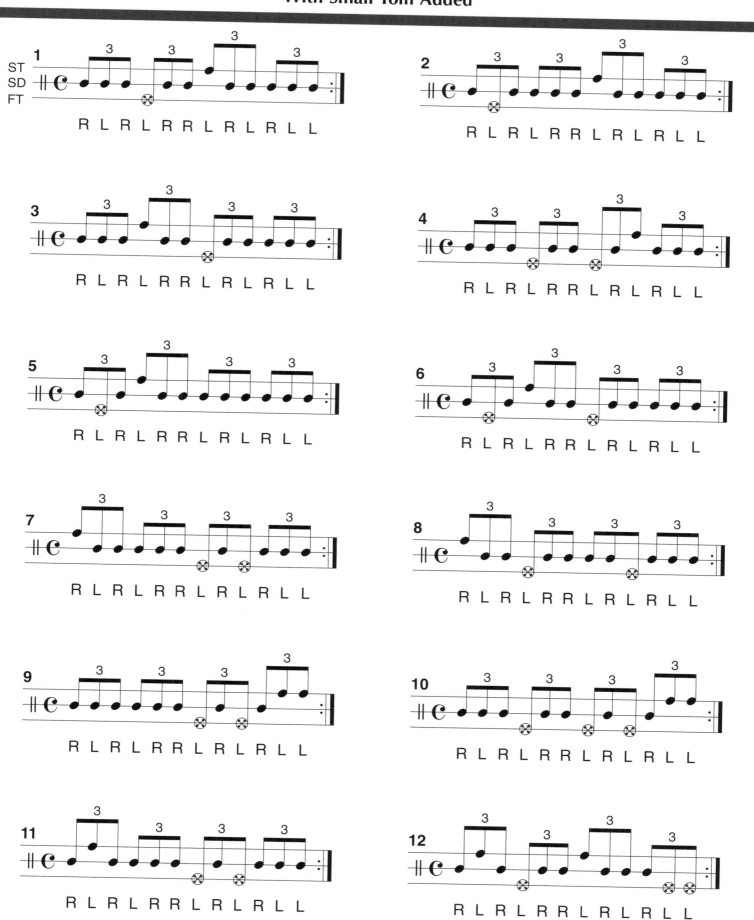

Floor Tom To Snare Drum With Right Hand Crossing Over Left

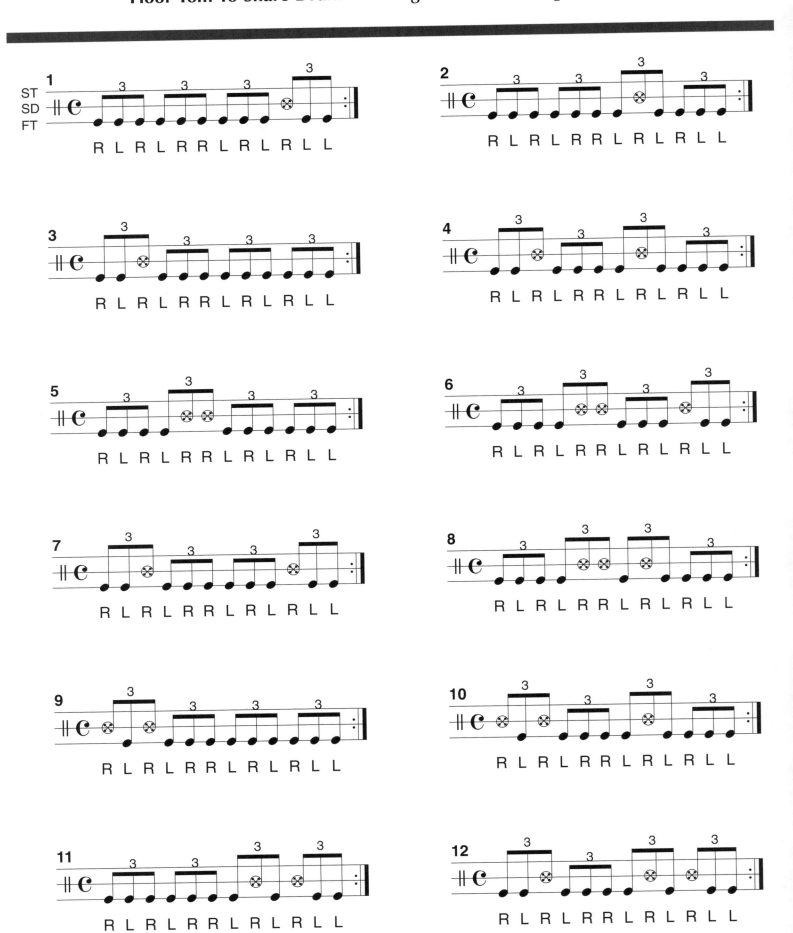

Floor Tom To Snare Drum (Right Hand Crossing Over Left)
With Small Tom Added

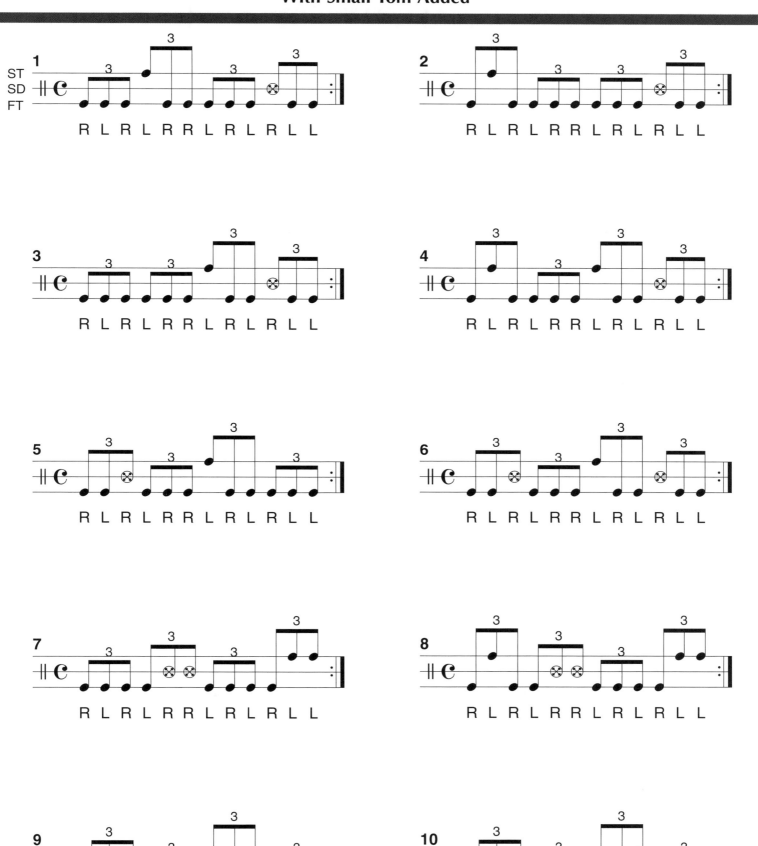

Small Tom To Floor Tom With Left Hand Crossing Over Right

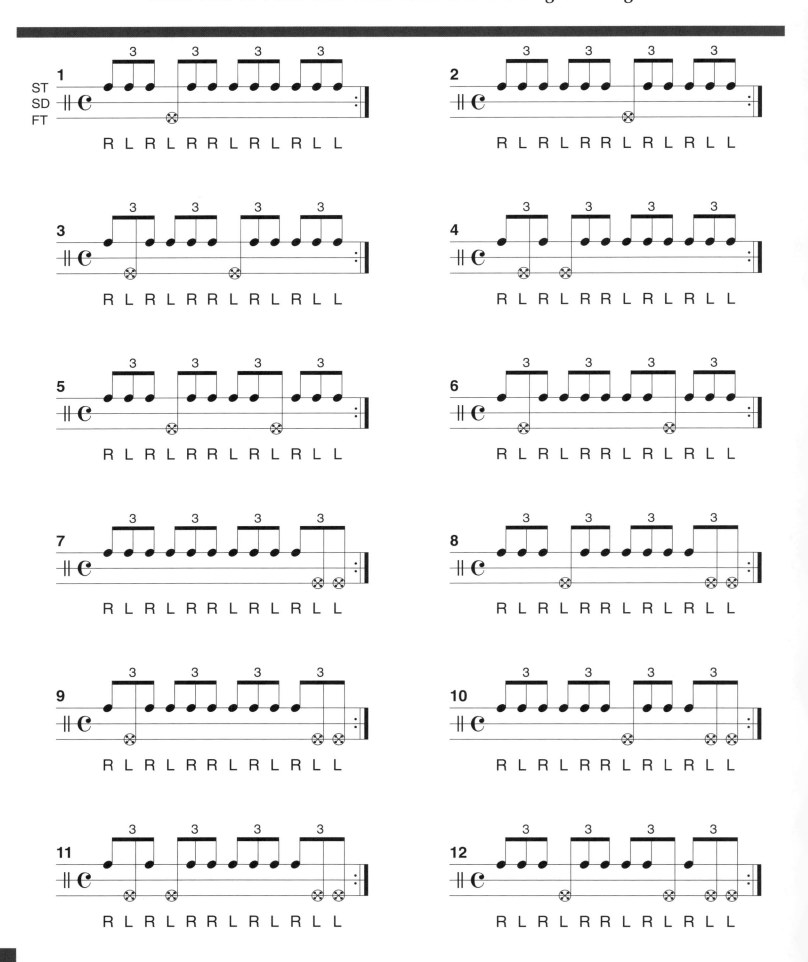

Small Tom To Floor Tom (Left Hand Crossing Over Right)
With Snare Drum Added

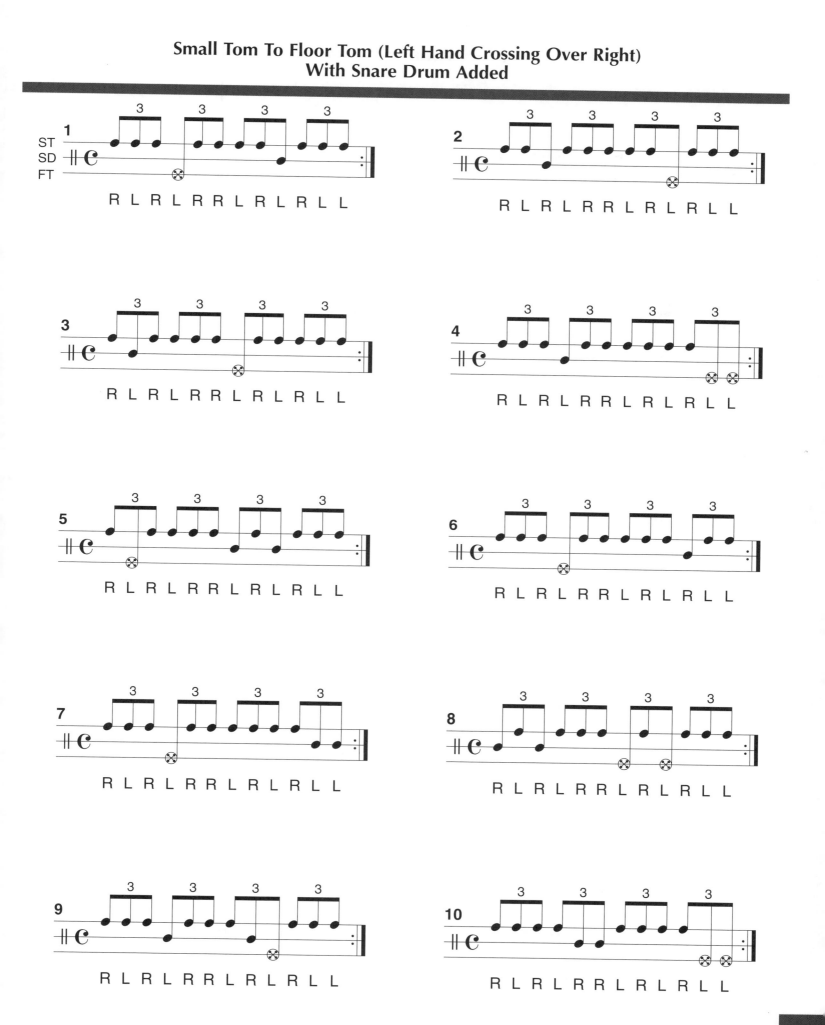

Floor Tom To Small Tom With Right Hand Crossing Over Left

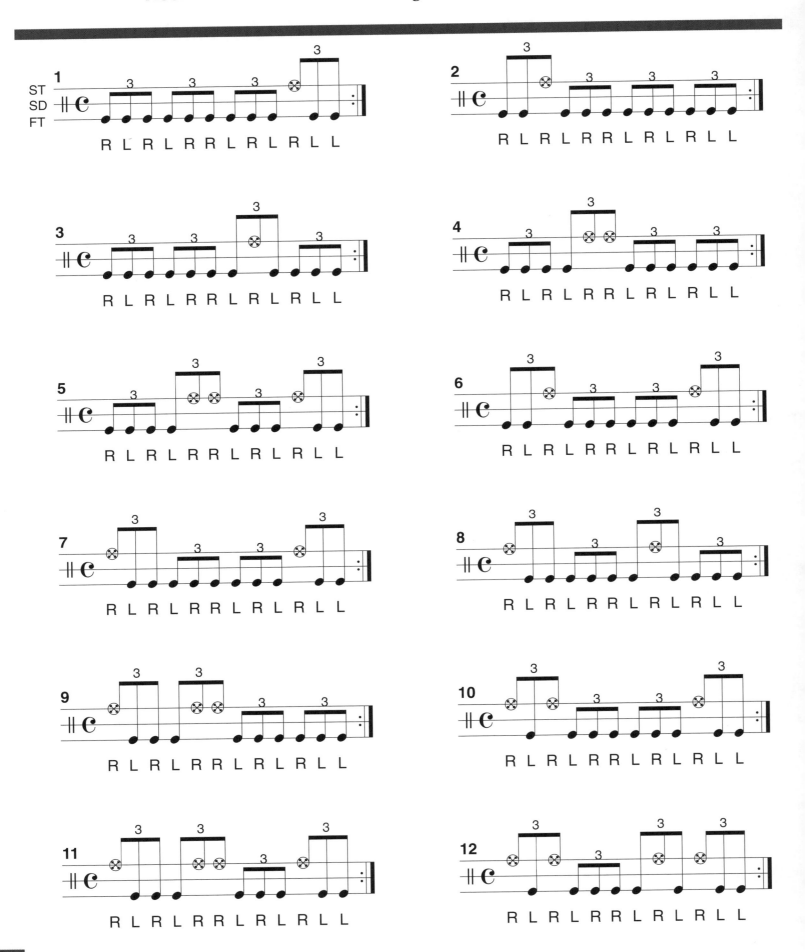

Floor Tom To Small Tom (Right Hand Crossing Over Left)
With Snare Drum Added

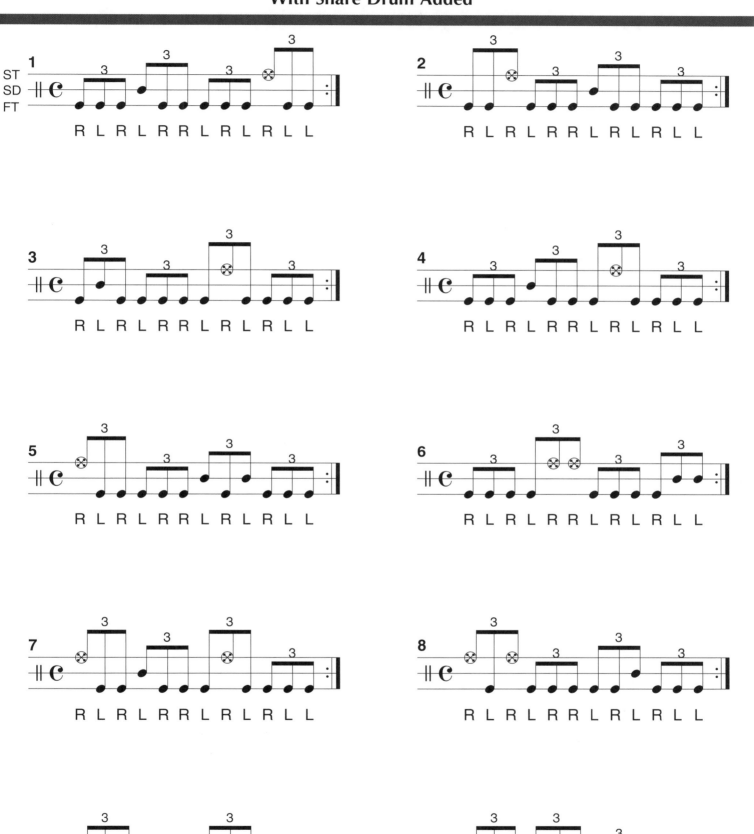

Two-Bar Combinations

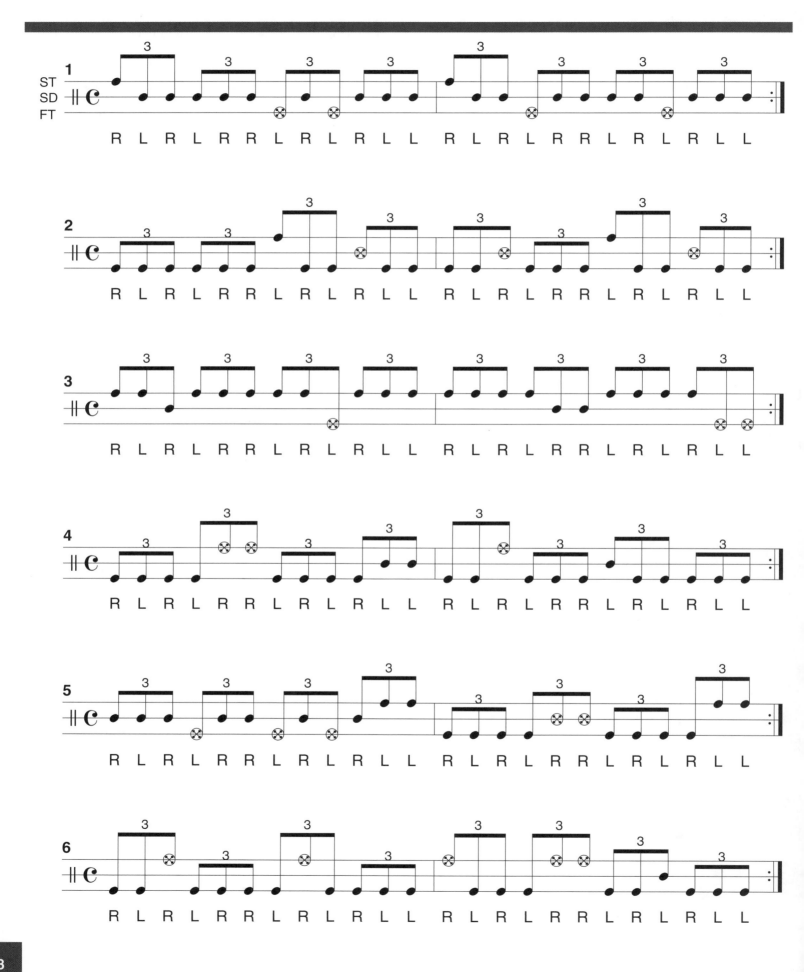

PART 3: TRIPLET PATTERNS USING RLL STICKING

Snare Drum To Floor Tom With Left Hand Crossing Over Right

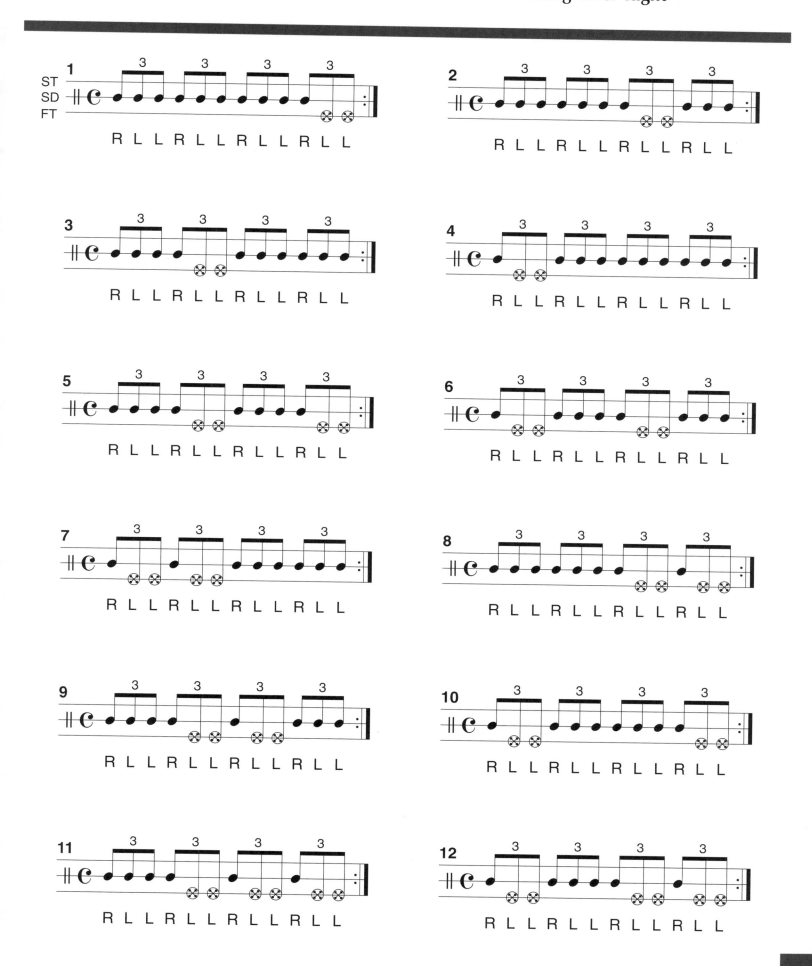

Snare Drum To Floor Tom (Left Hand Crossing Over Right)
With Small Tom Added

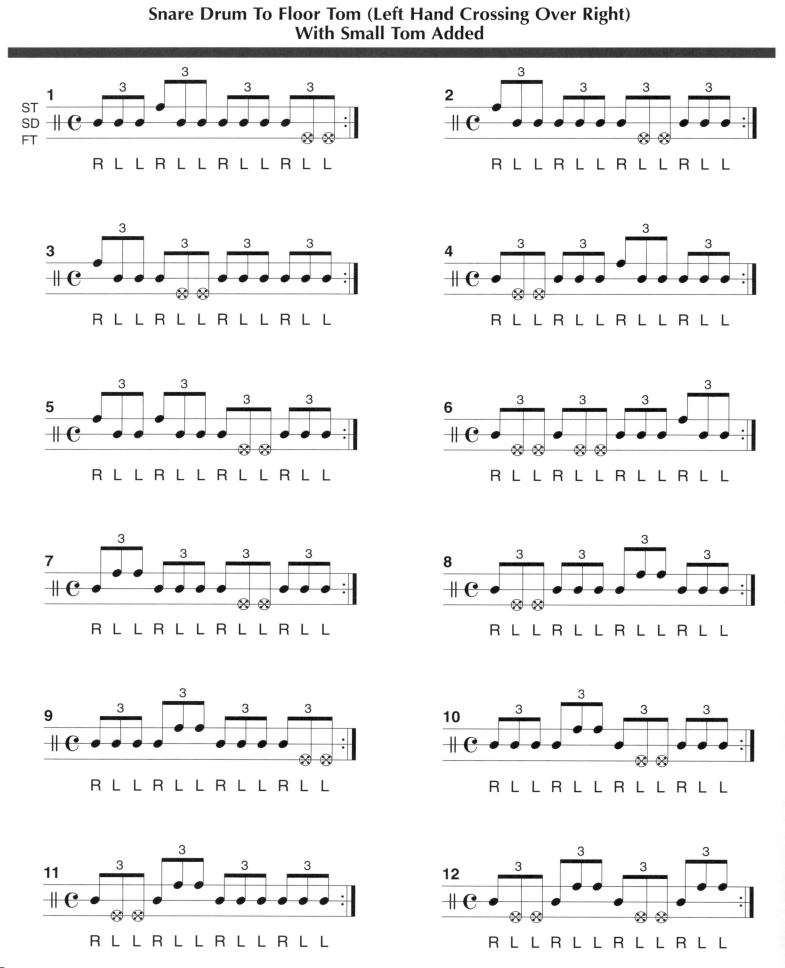

Floor Tom To Snare Drum With Right Hand Crossing Over Left

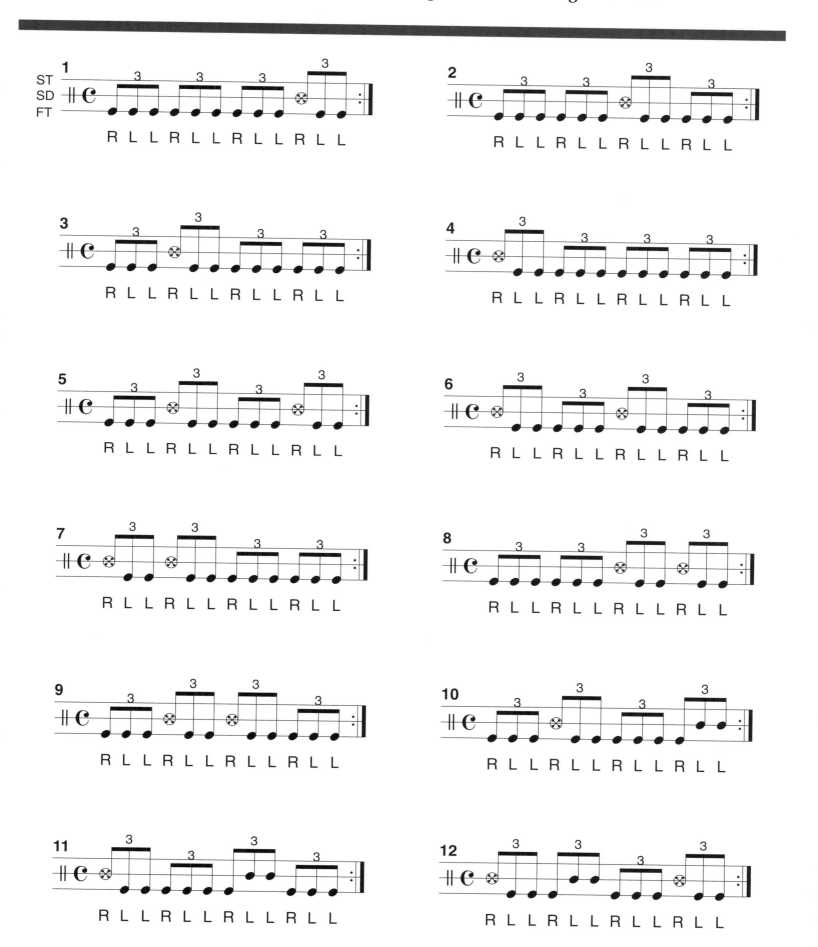

Floor Tom To Snare Drum (Right Hand Crossing Over Left)
With Small Tom Added

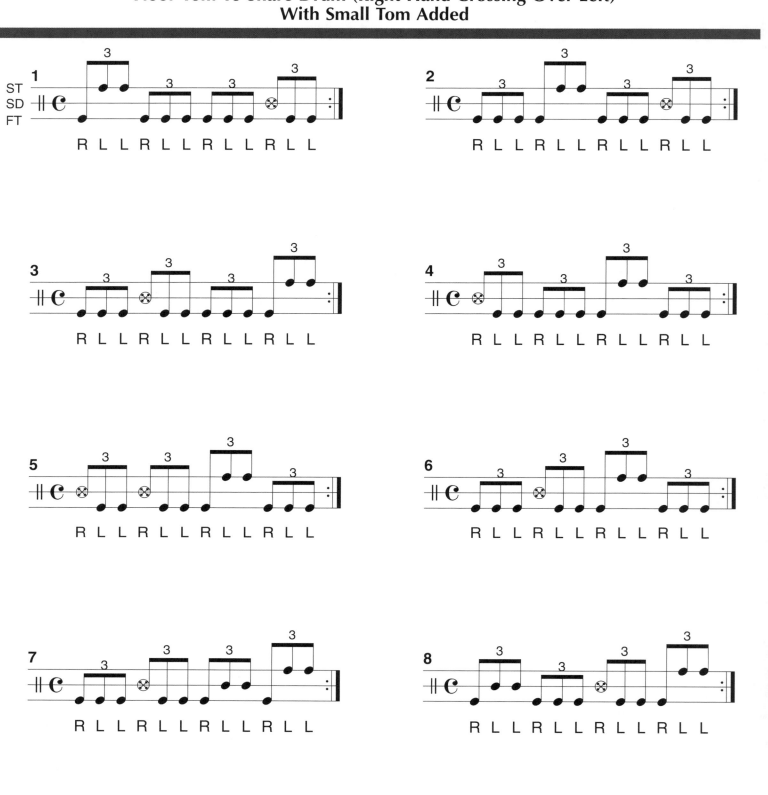

Small Tom To Floor Tom With Left Hand Crossing Over Right

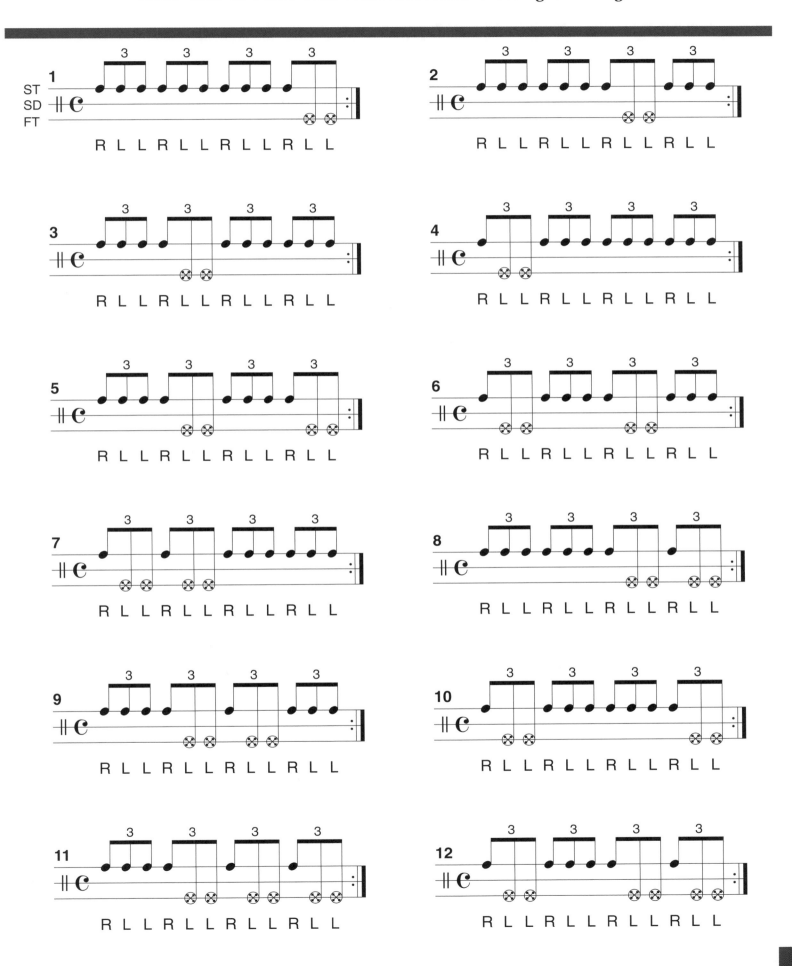

Small Tom To Floor Tom (Left Hand Crossing Over Right)
With Snare Drum Added

Floor Tom To Small Tom With Right Hand Crossing Over Left

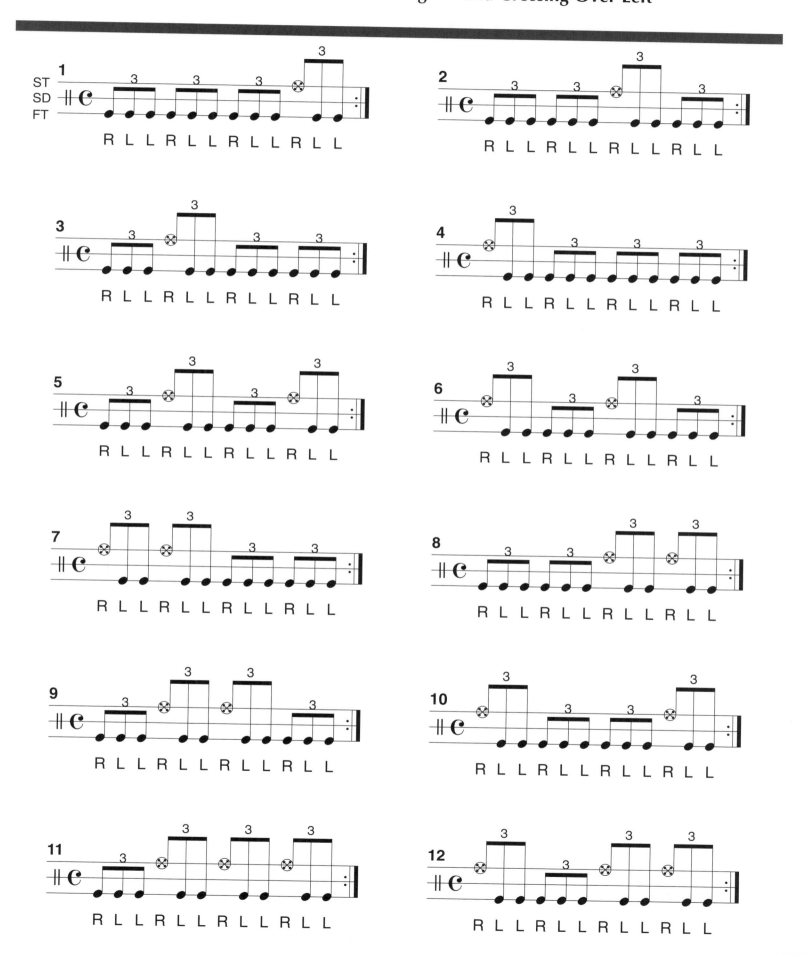

Floor Tom To Small Tom (Right Hand Crossing Over Left)
With Snare Drum Added

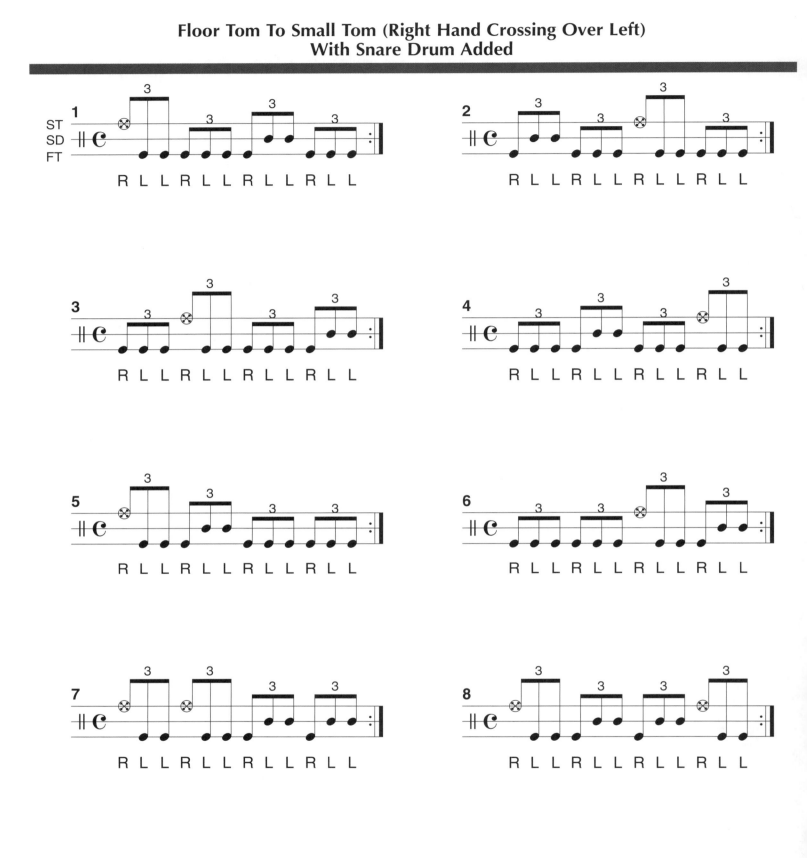

66

Two-Bar Combinations

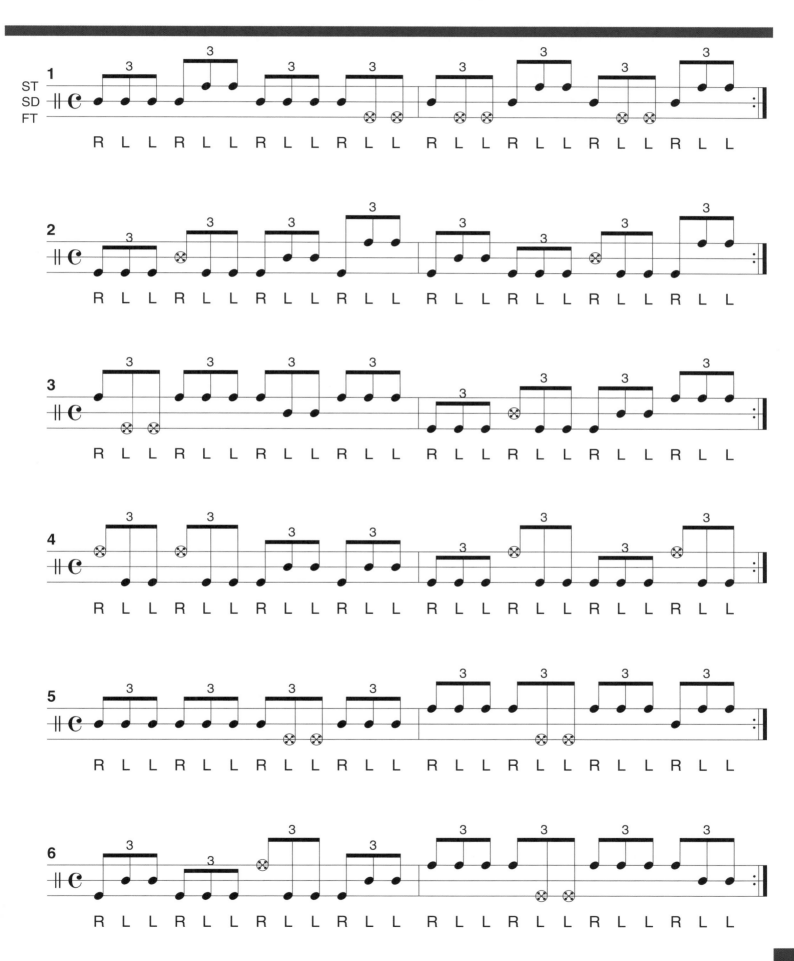

PART 4: TRIPLET PATTERNS USING LRR STICKING

Snare Drum To Floor Tom With Left Hand Crossing Over Right

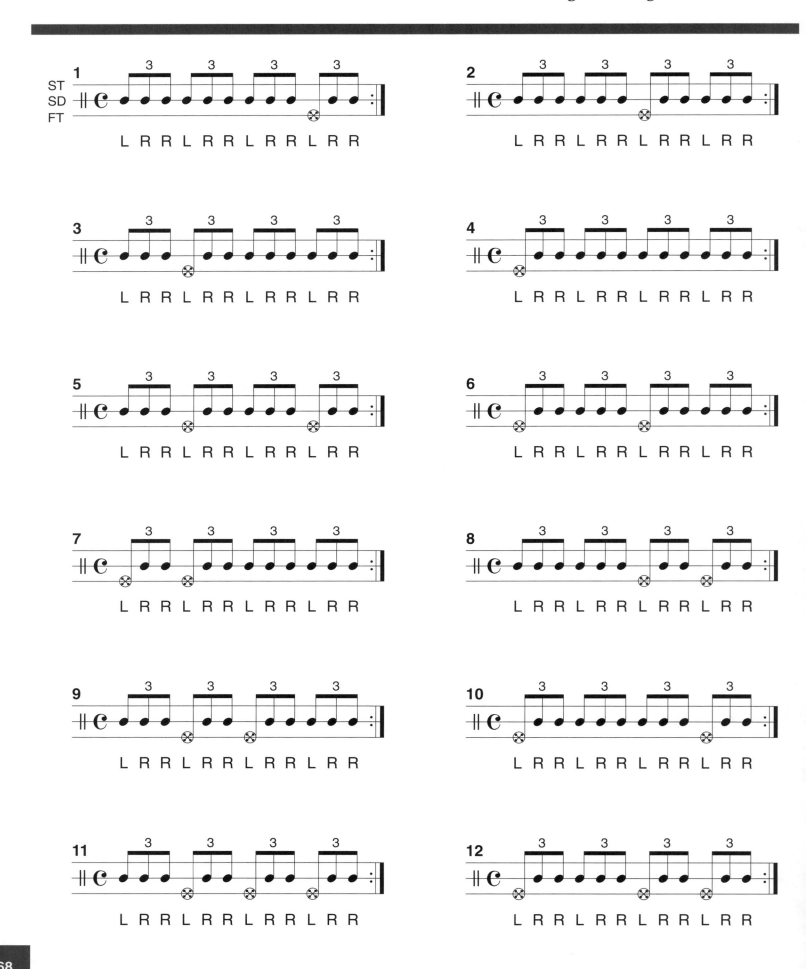

Snare Drum To Floor Tom (Left Hand Crossing Over Right)
With Small Tom Added

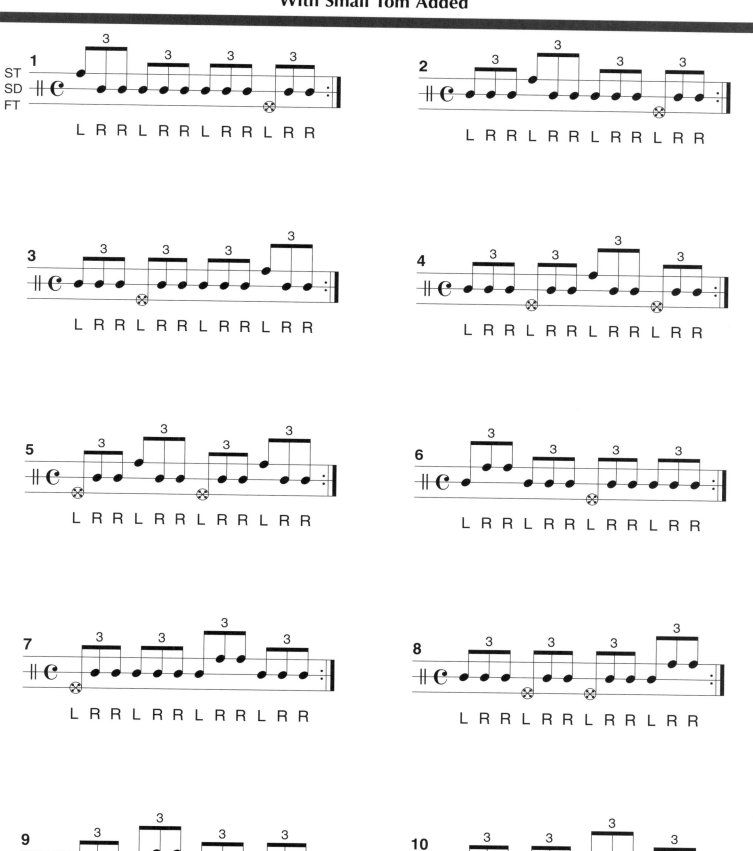

Floor Tom To Snare Drum With Right Hand Crossing Over Left

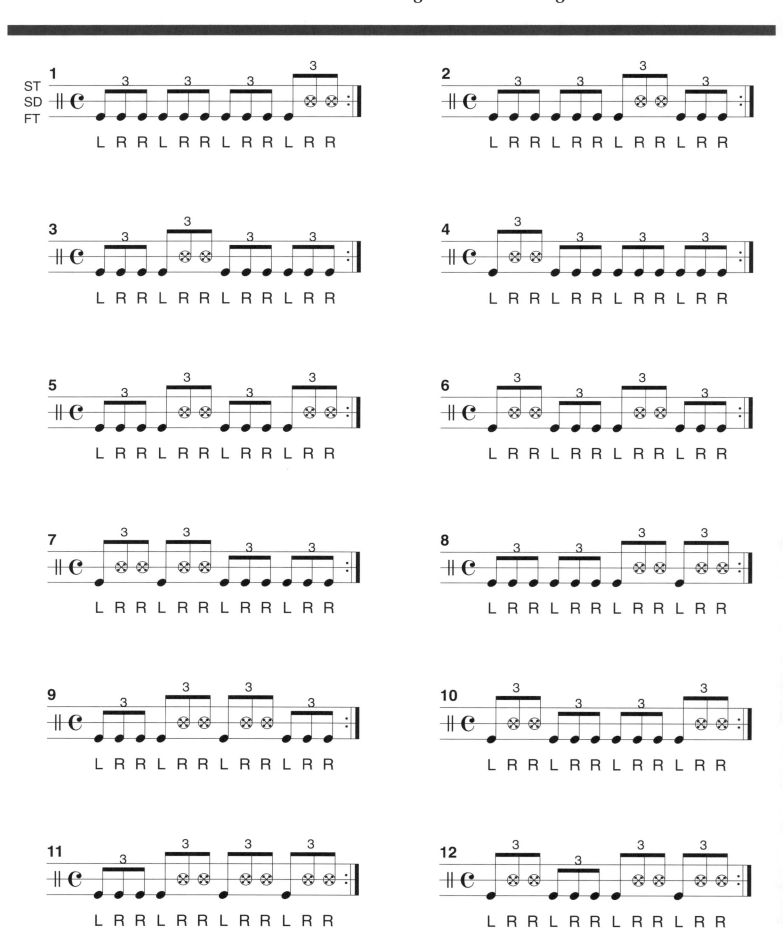

Floor Tom To Snare Drum (Right Hand Crossing Over Left)
With Small Tom Added

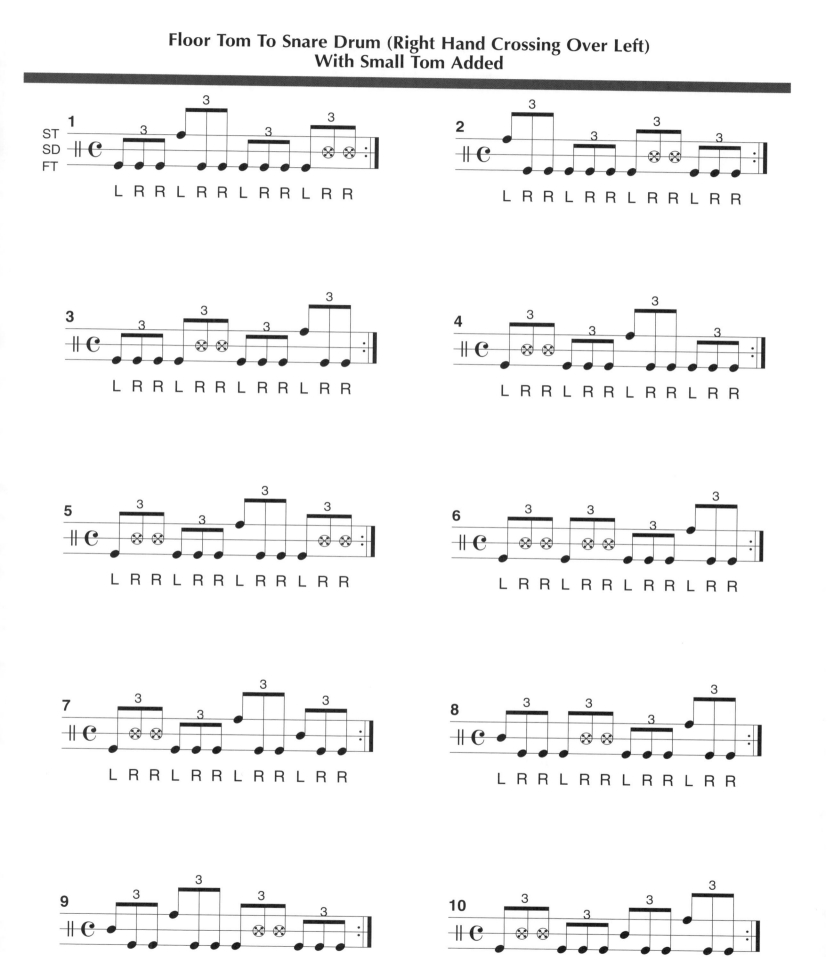

Small Tom To Floor Tom With Left Hand Crossing Over Right

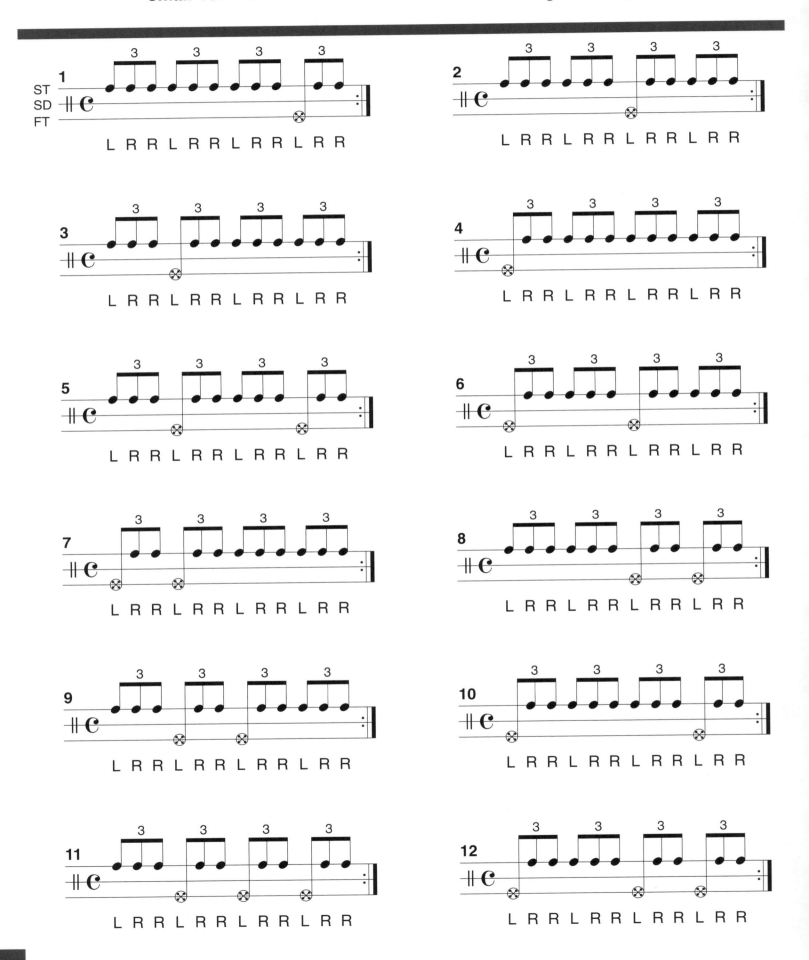

Small Tom To Floor Tom (Left Hand Crossing Over Right)
With Snare Drum Added

Floor Tom To Small Tom With Right Hand Crossing Over Left

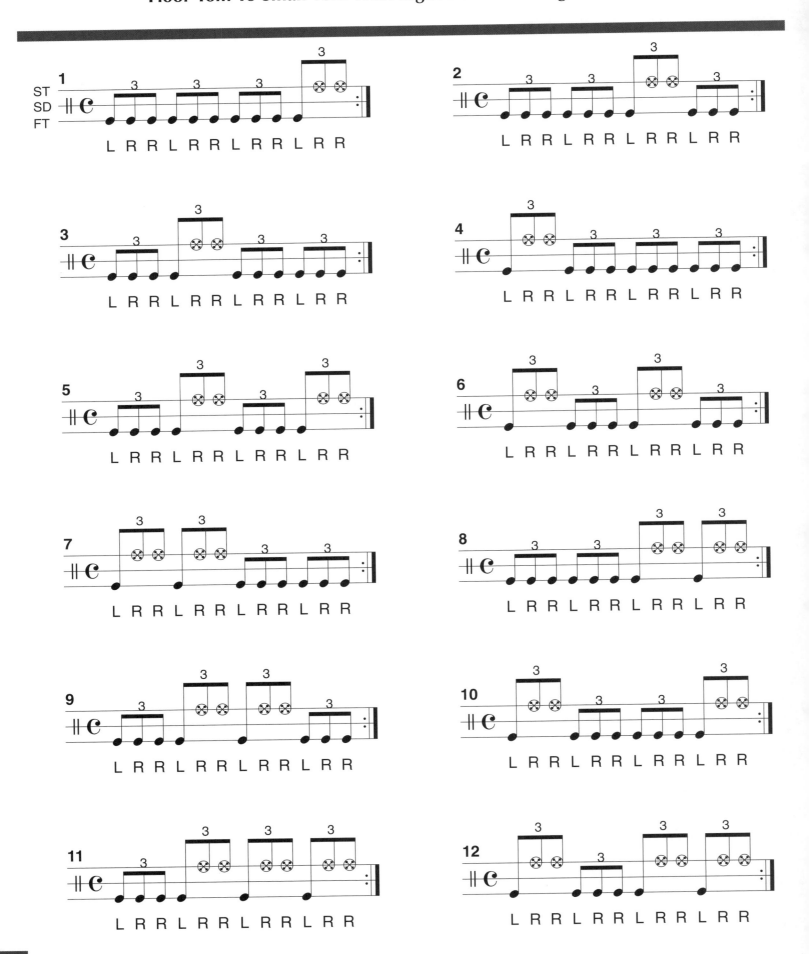

Floor Tom To Small Tom (Right Hand Crossing Over Left)
With Snare Drum Added

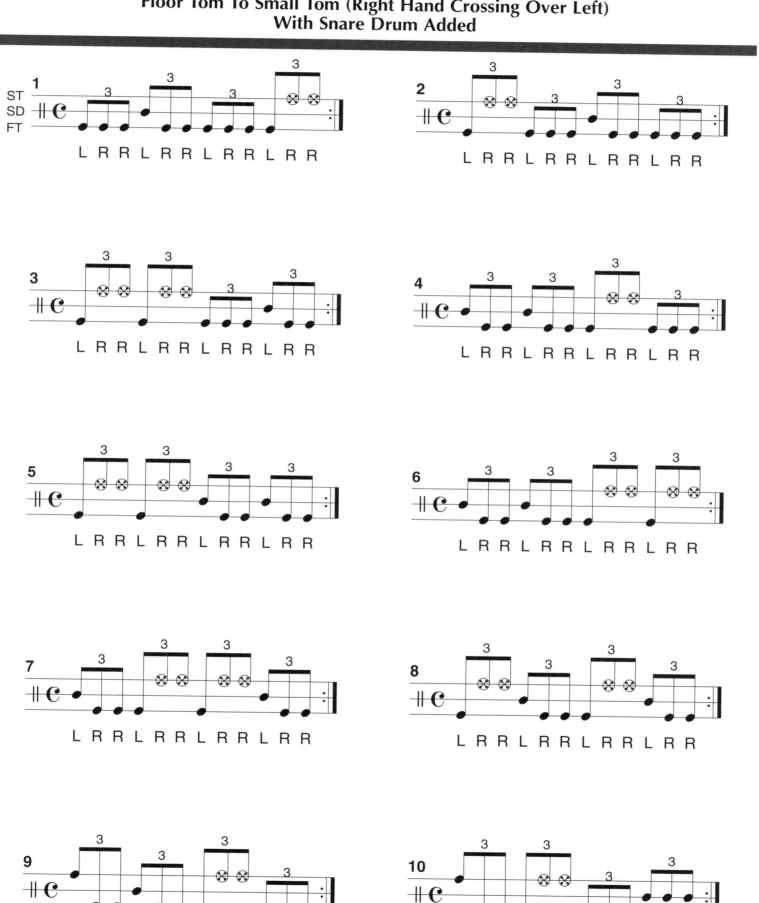

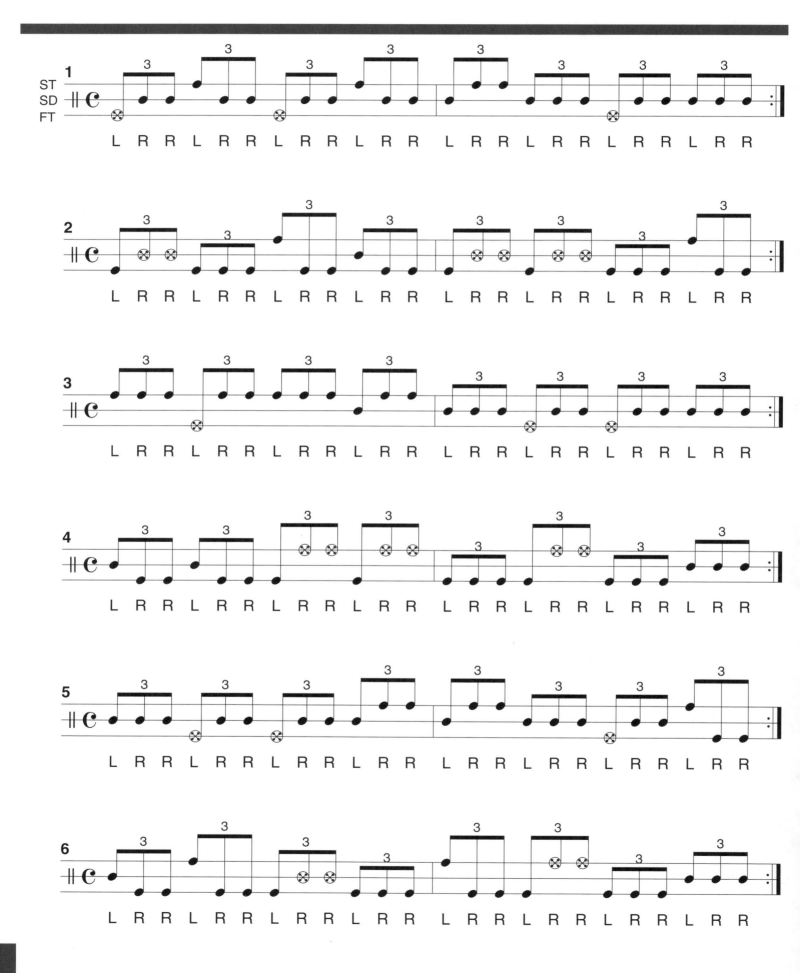

PART 5: TRIPLET PATTERNS USING RRL STICKING

Snare Drum To Floor Tom With Left Hand Crossing Over Right

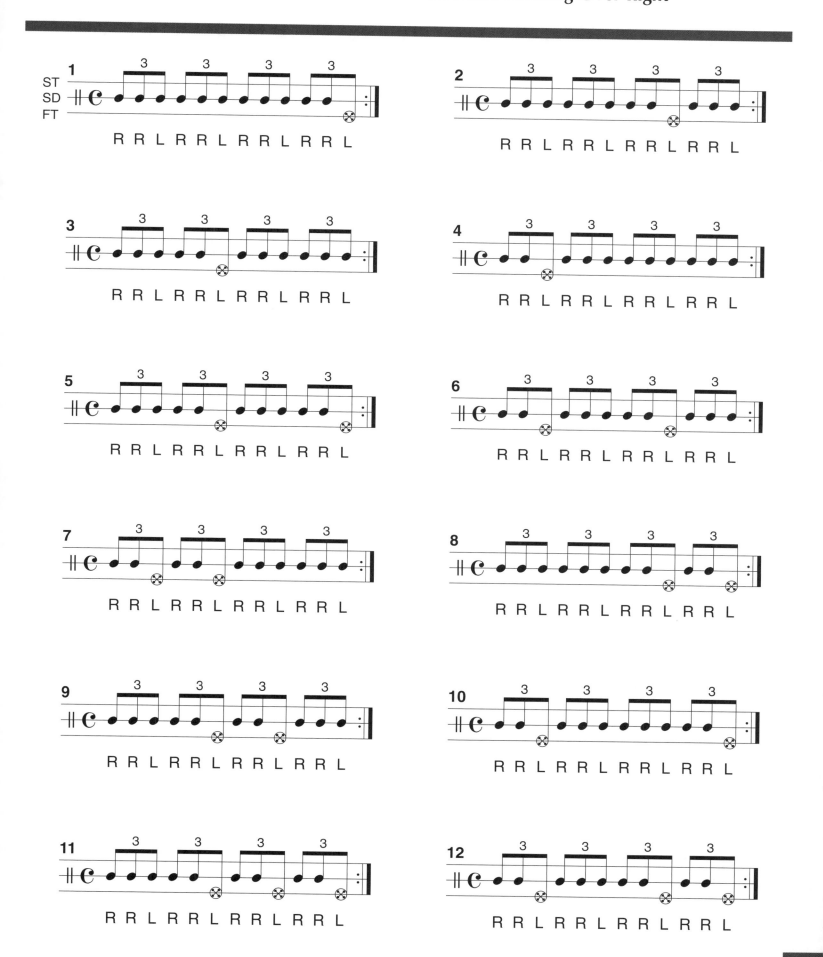

Snare Drum To Floor Tom (Left Hand Crossing Over Right)
With Small Tom Added

Floor Tom To Snare Drum With Right Hand Crossing Over Left

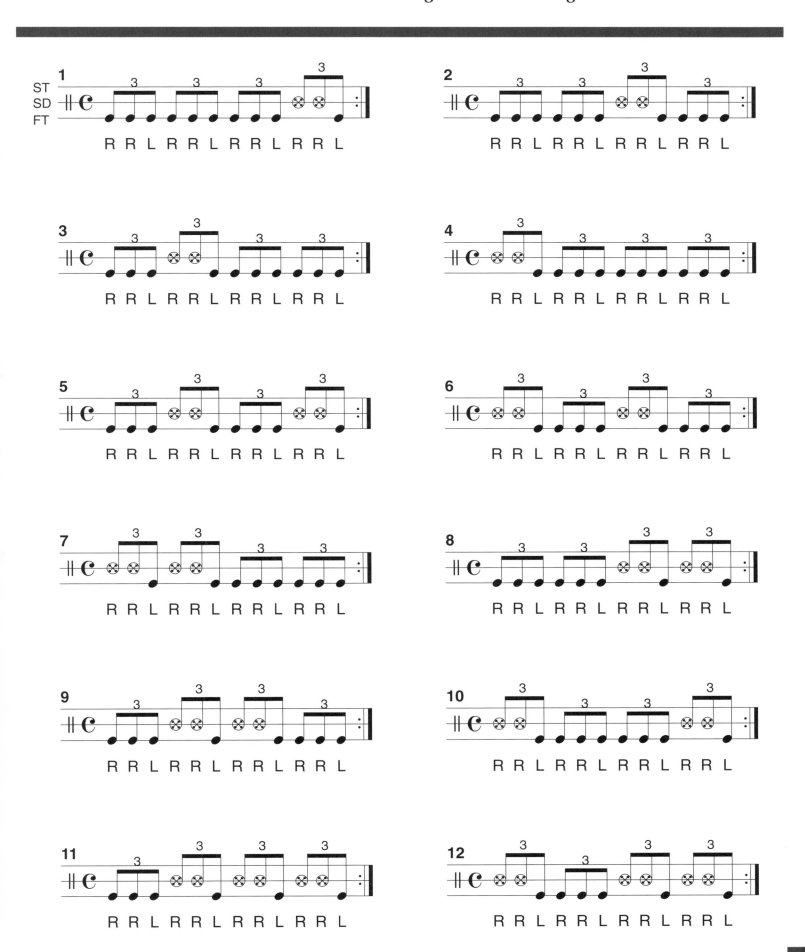

Floor Tom To Snare Drum (Right Hand Crossing Over Left)
With Small Tom Added

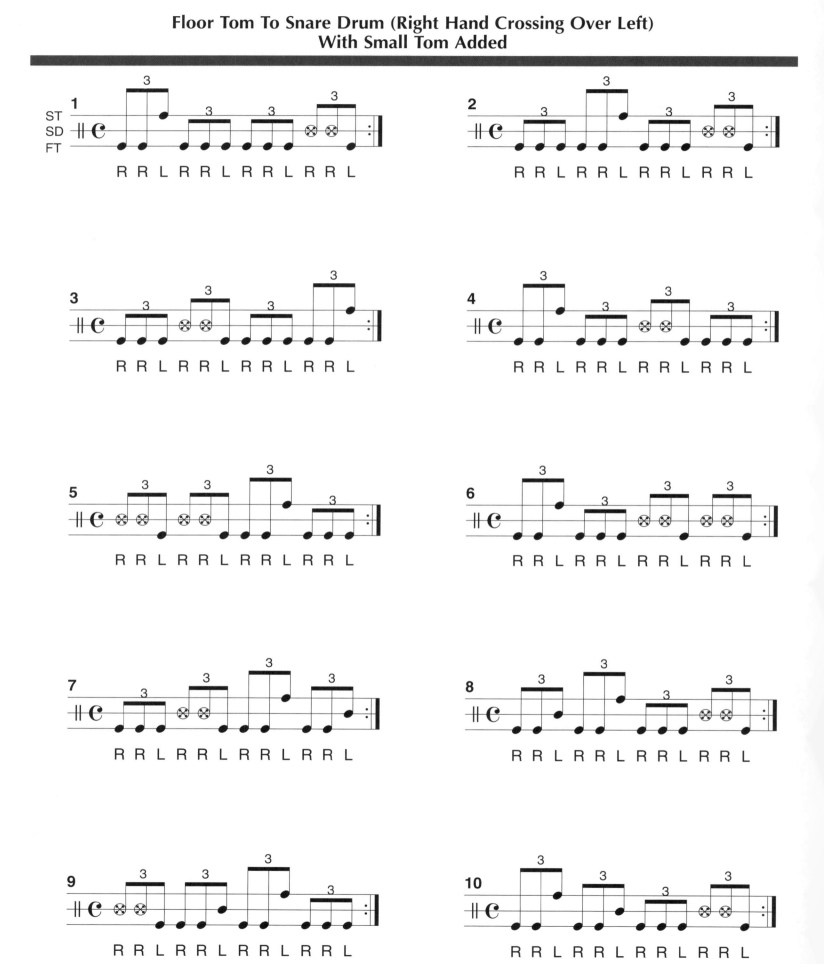

Small Tom To Floor Tom With Left Hand Crossing Over Right

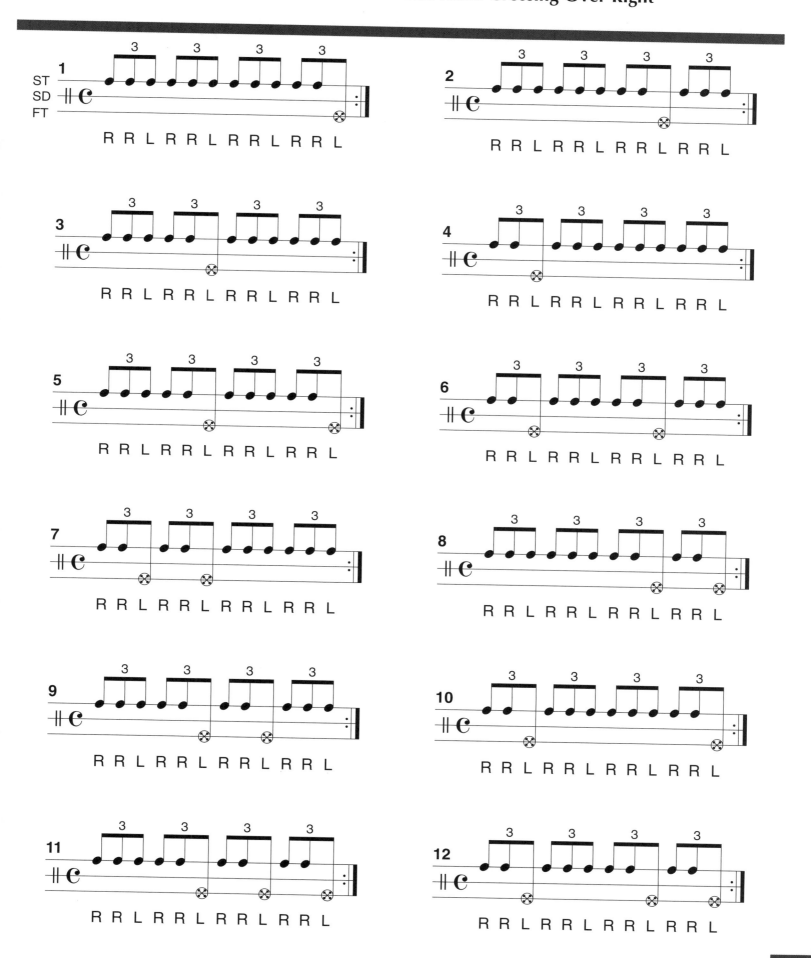

Small Tom To Floor Tom (Left Hand Crossing Over Right)
With Snare Drum Added

Floor Tom To Small Tom With Right Hand Crossing Over Left

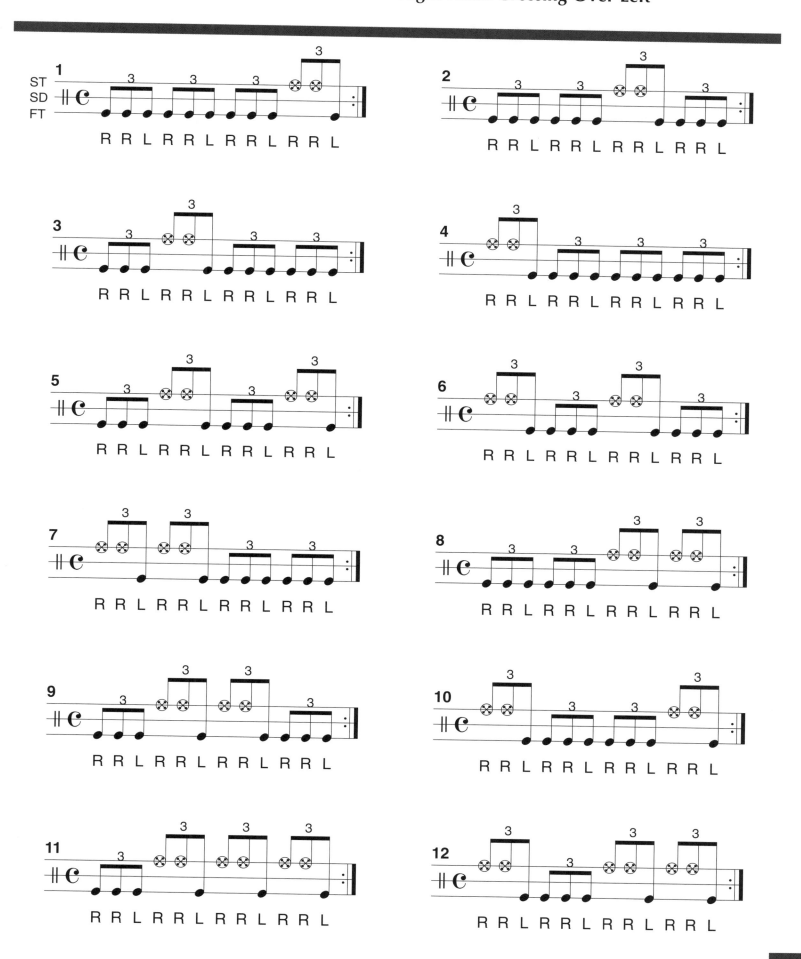

Floor Tom To Small Tom (Right Hand Crossing Over Left)
With Snare Drum Added

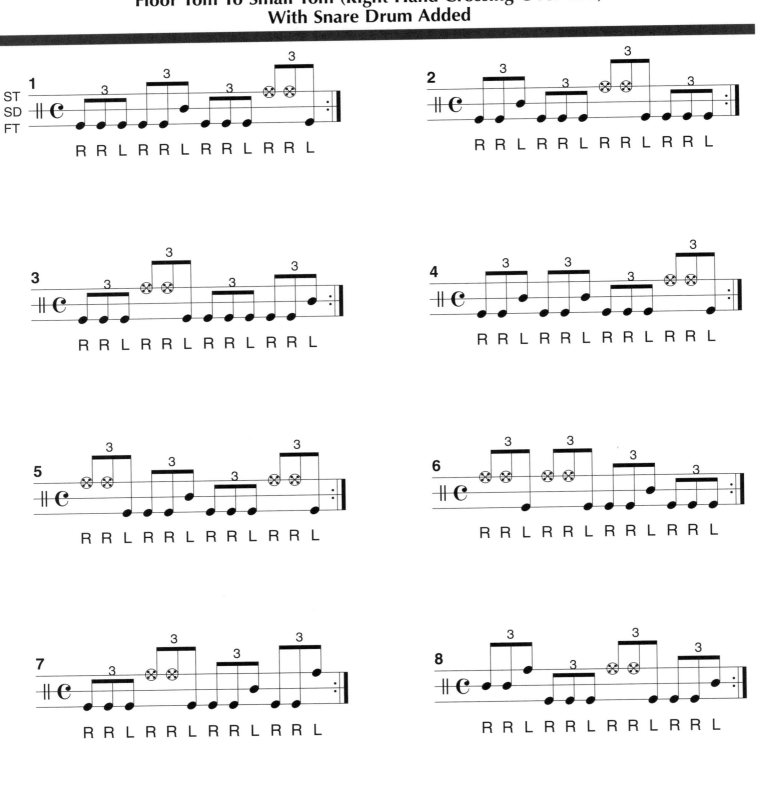

Two-Bar Combinations

PART 6: TRIPLET PATTERNS USING LLR STICKING

Snare Drum To Floor Tom With Left Hand Crossing Over Right

Snare Drum To Floor Tom (Left Hand Crossing Over Right)
With Small Tom Added

Floor Tom To Snare Drum With Right Hand Crossing Over Left

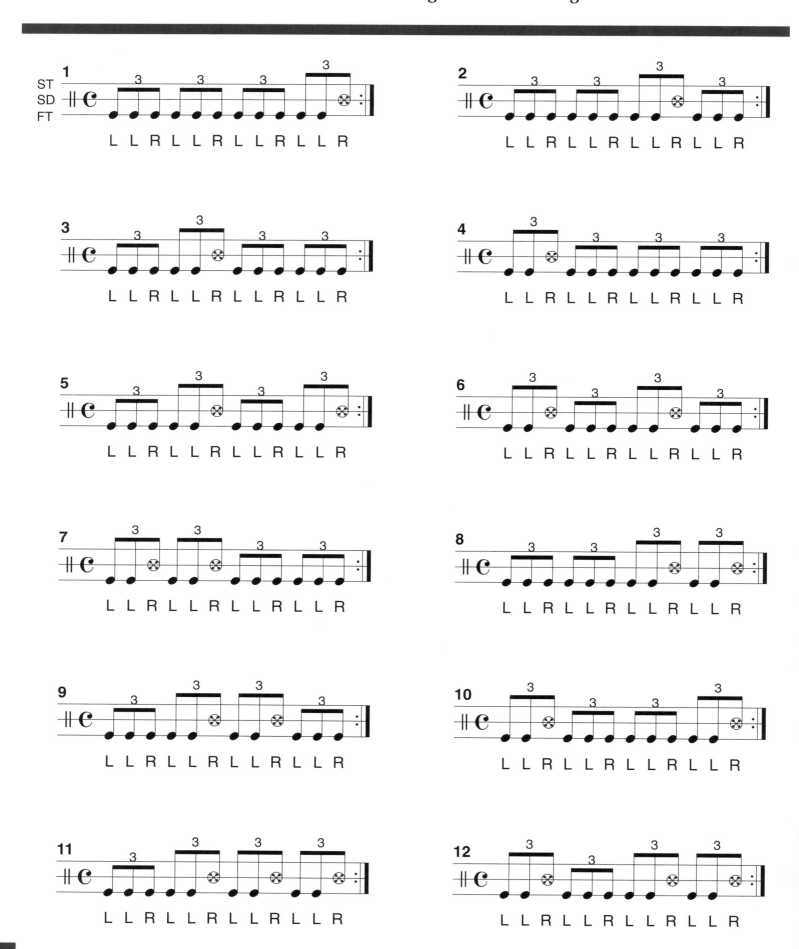

Floor Tom To Snare Drum (Right Hand Crossing Over Left)
With Small Tom Added

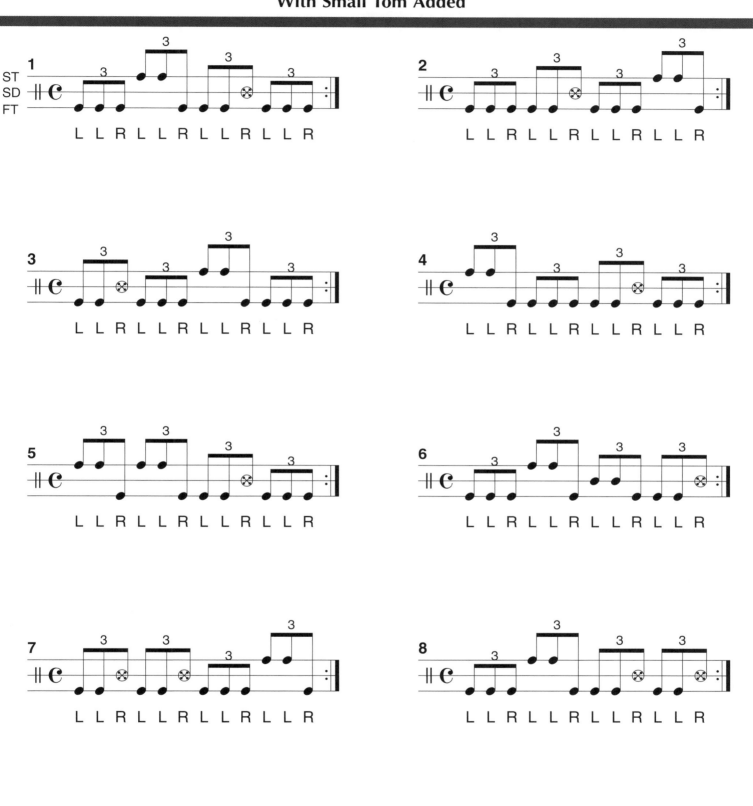

Small Tom To Floor Tom With Left Hand Crossing Over Right

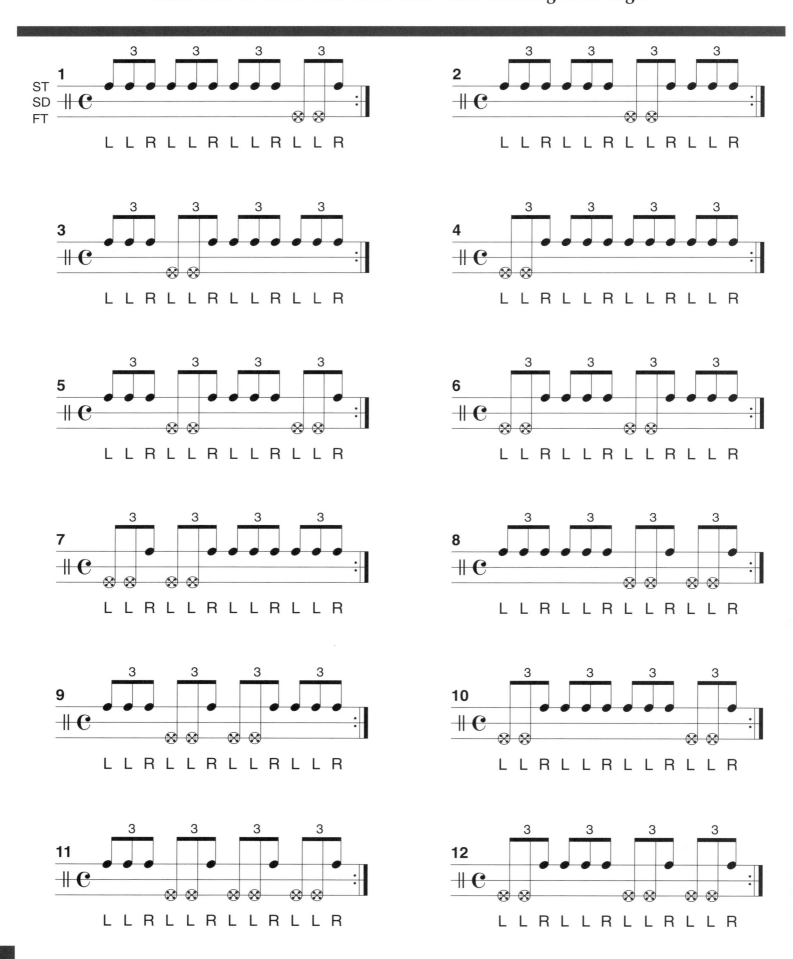

Small Tom To Floor Tom (Left Hand Crossing Over Right)
With Snare Drum Added

Floor Tom To Small Tom With Right Hand Crossing Over Left

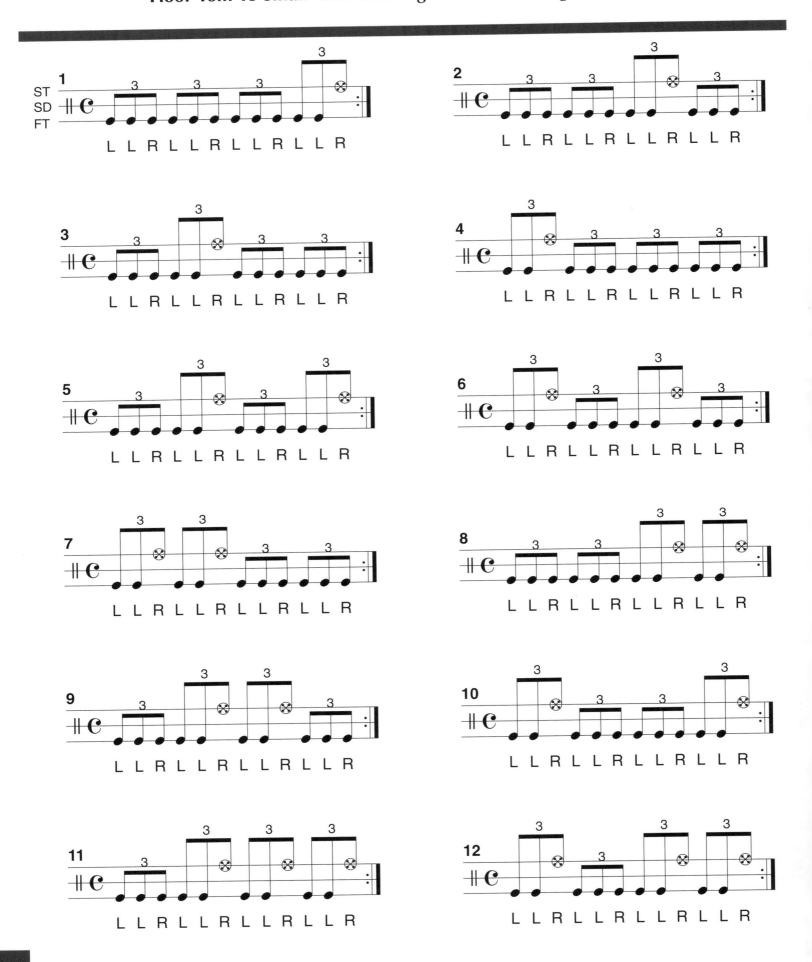

92

Floor Tom To Small Tom (Right Hand Crossing Over Left)
With Snare Drum Added

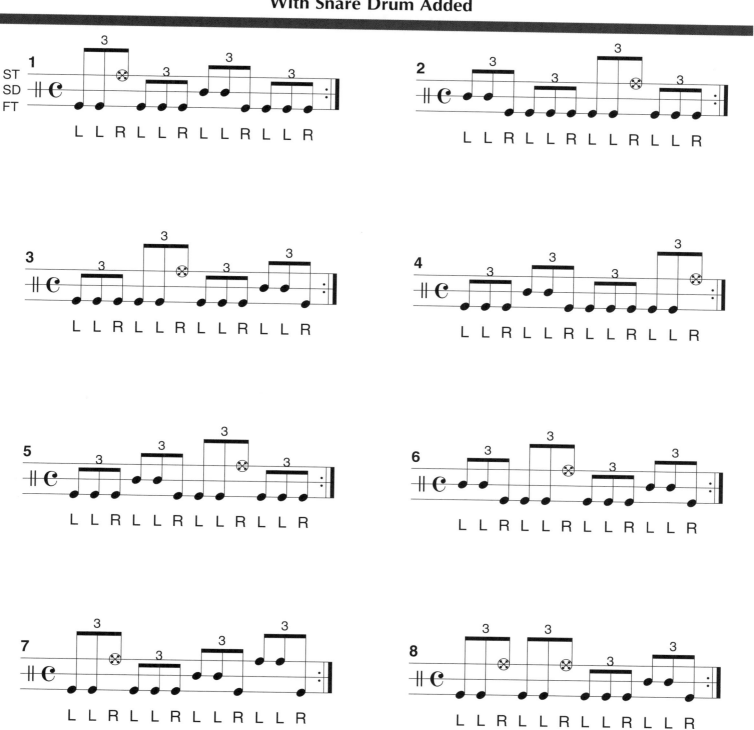

PART 7: TWO-BAR COMBINATIONS WITH MIXED STICKING

Note that the sticking pattern changes in the second bar of each of the following exercises. Be sure to play each two-bar sticking pattern several times on just the snare drum, before adding the cross-sticking moves.

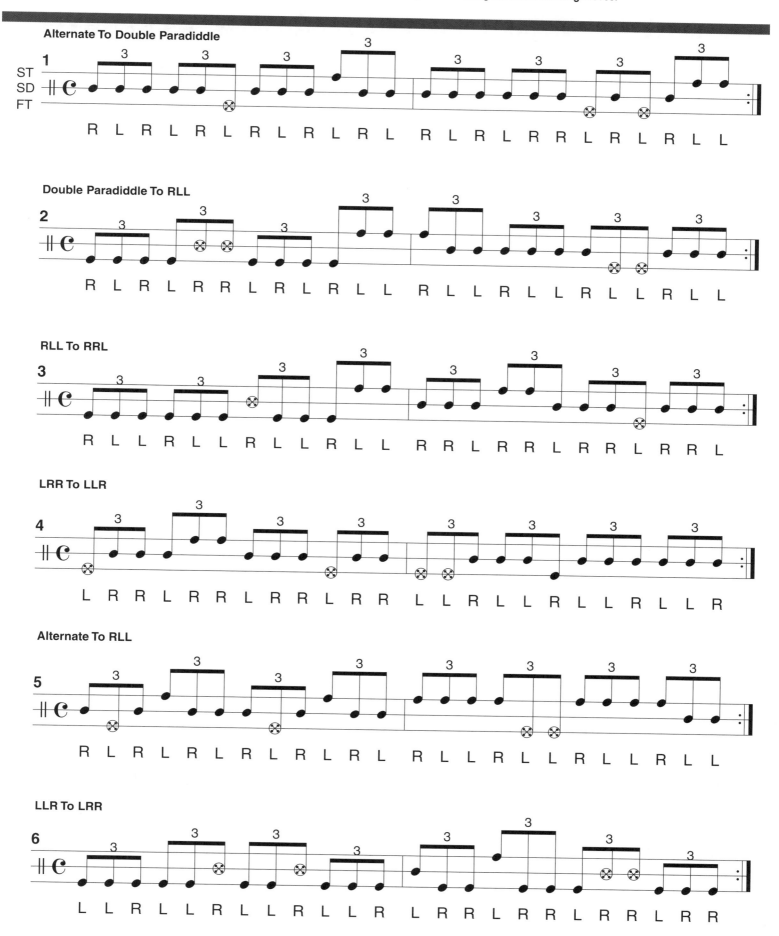

Alternate To Double Paradiddle

1

R L R L R L R L R L R L   R L R L R R L R L R L L

Double Paradiddle To RLL

2

R L R L R R L R L R L L   R L L R L L R L L R L L

RLL To RRL

3

R L L R L L R L L R L L   R R L R R L R R L R R L

LRR To LLR

4

L R R L R R L R R L R R   L L R L L R L L R L L R

Alternate To RLL

5

R L R L R L R L R L R L   R L L R L L R L L R L L

LLR To LRR

6

L L R L L R L L R L L R   L R R L R R L R R L R R

95